Complete Book of
Triple Option Football

Complete Book of
Triple Option Football

Jack Olcott

Parker Publishing Company, Inc.

West Nyack, N.Y.

Library of Congress Cataloging in Publication Data

Olcott, Jack.
   Complete book of triple option football.

   Includes index.
   1. Football--Offense. I. Title.
GV951.8.039   796.33'22   75-14067
ISBN 0-13-158089-2

Other Books By the Author

Football Coach's Guide to Successful Pass Defense
Coaching the Quarterback
Football's Fabulous Forty Defense

How This Book Will Help You

The Triple Option play is the most explosive, scientifically designed, and strategically oriented play ever made in football. This diversified maneuver gives the quarterback the option of attacking six points along the line of scrimmage. The Triple Option play enables the quarterback to hand the ball off, pitch it out, or keep the ball after having actually read the defender's charges after the ball has been put into play. This play can be run from either a two or three back offensive backfield set. Thus, the Triple Optioning offense dictates to the defense that they must be lined up in a balanced defense or accept the consequences.

The Triple Option play often freezes the defender on the line of scrimmage because of the three-way faking by the Triple Optioning backs. The freezing of an individual defender often results in an explosive play. Many defensive teams assign specific defenders to stop either the dive man, the quarterback keeper, or the wide pitchout threat. A mental or physical mistake by any one of these assigned defenders often results in the long home run play. The simplicity and consistency of this three dimensional maneuver limits the stunting effectiveness of the defense, because it forces the defense to reassign defenders to specific offensive personnel on the move. Therefore, the acutal point of the attack of the Triple Option play does not have to be determined until the defense actually commits itself.

Whenever the defense predetermines a particular defender responsible for the dive, pitchman, or keeper, this defender must commit himself to his offensive assignment, whether the offensive player has the ball or is merely a faker. Thus, the Triple Option greatly minimizes the defensive team's pursuit patterns.

This three way play affords the offensive flexibility to mesmerize the defense by combining the Triple Option play into an inside power play, an outside breakaway threat, or throwing the long bomb.

There is minimal use of the automatic call prior to the snap of the ball by the quarterback becuase the quarterback is able to read the defense after the ball has been put into play. Thus, the quarterback is able to read the defense on the move after the ball has been placed into play.

The Triple Option play always maintains the constant threat of the long pass because at least one wide receiver is flexed or split wide on each play. Yet, this three dimensional play is a devastating ground attack by itself and can be used successfully as a ball control offense. The Triple Option play is a high scoring offense which features long scoring strikes as well as a powerful scoring attack inside the opposition's ten yard line.

Just as the title implies, this book completely covers step by step progression of how to run the Triple Option attack from the Wishbone, "I", and Veer (two split backs) offensive formations. This "how to" guide is a most valuable book not only for the head coach and his staff, but is a necessary reading guide for all palyers from the quarterback to the offensive tackle. The primary reason for writing this book is to make both the coach and the players a more successful and knowledgable teacher and performer.

The chapter on "How to Coach the Triple Optioning Quarterback" is a descriptive discussion of how to successfully launch the famous three way maneuver. This is a must chapter for all aspiring, as well as the most seasoned, triple optioning quarterbacks on the squad. This chapter will tell the quarterback how, when, and why to step, read, fake, and option each individual defender.

Chapter 5 explains the offensive line's blocking techniques and line blocking rules. The line blocking rules are easy to execute, and the blockers have excellent blocking angles because only the interior defenders, inside of the offensive tackles, must be blocked. Thus, the interior offensive line screens or seals off the defensive inside persuit so that smooth execution by the quarterback allows the ball carrier a solid chance to turn the corner for the long gainer. This chapter also covers all blocking techniques from the split end's run off block to the center's option blocking techniques.

This book tells how the Triple Option play can be run from the three back Wishbone, two stacked "I", and split back Veer formations. Along with the Triple Option explosive running attack, the author also explains how to include the play action "Pop Pass,"

Counter Bomb, and throw-back passes which fit smoothly into the total offensive package.

The most successful pass patterns are discussed and diagrammed from the "I", Veer, and Wishbone formations. These scoring patterns are described from the straight drop back, sprint, and play action maneuvers.

The newest offensive method for numbering the defensive players and how to identify and read the all-important inside and outside defensive keys are diagrammed and described clearly so the reader will learn in a step-by-step progression.

"How to Coach the I Triple Option" covers such topics as fold blocking, how to attack the rolling secondary, and how to coach the wide receiver's sprint off block.

This book teaches the reader how the offensive backfield smoothly executes blocking the crashing as well as the "feathering" contain man, how the fullback is coached to make the most effective fake as well as shoot the crease for the big gaining quick opener, and how the pitchman should set up the lead block to turn the corner against a variety of defensive alignments.

All of the Triple Option running maneuvers are covered in detail from the simplest fullback dive play to the "razzle-dazzle" end around play. All of these plays have been described and illustrated in charts and diagrmas throughout this book. The author goes into detail to describe how to block and take apart the various two, three and four deep secondary defenses.

This text also described how the reader may incorporate the drive option, counter option, and trap series into his offensive attack.

This Triple Option attack is able to advantageously use the full width and depth of the gridiron to score at any time or from any place.

Jack Olcott

Contents

3   How to Coach the Triple Option Quarterback *(cont.)*

–Second Point of Decision
–Quarterback's Ride Fake
–Faking Quarterback
–Altering the Collision Path
–The Quarterback Keeper
–The Keeper Technique
–If In Doubt, Keep the Ball
–Keep the Ball Versus a #4 Technique Defender
–Ball Adjustment Prior to the Pitch
–Pitch Out First, Keep Only When Forced
–Quarterback's Pitch Out
–Timing the Pitch Out
–The Quick Triple Option Pitch
–Left Handed Pitch
–How To Pitch On the Run
–How To Absorb the Blow After the Pitch
–How to Read the Dive Key (Wishbone, "I," Veer)
–How to Read the Pitch Key

4   Wishbone's Triple Option Backfield Techniques • 47

–Fullback's Stance and Depth
–Fullback's Course
–The Crease
–Fullback's Pocket
–Fullback's Leveled Off Approach
–Fullback's Triple Option Assignment
–Lead Halfback's Stance and Depth
–Lead Blocker's Route and Techniques
–Lead Halfback's Block
–Lead Back's Blocking Techniques
–Blocking the Feathering Defender
–Lead Back's Kick Out Block
–Pitchman's Stance and Depth
–Pitchman's Assignment
–Halfback's Triple Option Paths
–Turning the Corner

5   Triple Option Line Blocking Techniques • 58

–Split End's Triple Option Assignment
–Split End's Block
–Frontside Tackle's Triple Option Blocking Techniques
–Playside Tackle
–Frontside Tackle's Triple Option "Looks"

5 Triple Option Line Blocking Techniques *(cont.)*

6 How to Run the Wishbone's Triple Option • 78

7 How to Block the Deep Secondaries • 101

8 The Drive Play • 111

Complete Book of
Triple Option Football

CHAPTER ONE

The Triple Option and

Its Explosive Formations

The Triple Option play, the most explosive play in football today, forces the defense to assign defenders to specific offensive players. One missed defensive assignment usually ends up in a long gainer or a possible touchdown; thus, the Triple Option attack forces all defenses to use a balanced defense. An overloaded defense may result in defensive chaos.

The three quaterback options allow the quarterback to direct the ball to six points along the line of scrimmage, after the ball has been put into play. Thus the quarterback is able to read the defender's techniques or blitzes and gives the ball off to the open offensive back.

The Triple Option can be run from a diversified selection of offensive formations using the Wishbone, "I," and Veer backfield sets. But, regardless whether the offensive formation features two split ends, or pro sets, the Triple Option play can still be run successfully.

Wishbone, "I" And Pro Veer Triple Option Series

This book illustrates and discusses the Triple Option running and passing plays from the Wishbone, "I," and Pro Veer formations. When discussing these formations, the Wishbone formation is described in Diagram 1-1, the "I" formation in Diagram 1-2, and the Pro Veer in Diagram 1-3.

While a more thorough description of the Wishbone Triple Option attack is featured, many of its Triple Option's assignments, fundamentals, and techniques may be applied to the "I" and Veer formations.

Since all three of these formations emphasize a particular phase of the Triple Option Series, the author has placed emphasis on each formation's strongest assets.

What Is The Triple Option?

Basically the offensive linemen block or wall off all of the interior defenders, leaving two outside defenders on or near the line of scrimmage. (Diagram 1-4.) The dive back (fullback in the Wishbone and "I") runs a course just outside of the outside foot of the frontside or playside offensive guard. The quarterback gives the dive man the ball if the first or dive key (circled) steps to his outside or steps across the line of scrimmage. (Diagrams 1-5, 1-6, and 1-7.) This is referred to as the first option.

If the first or dive key (circled) attacks the dive man (fullback in the Wishbone and "I"), the quarterback pulls the ball out and attacks the second, pitch or keeper, key (squared), If the squared defender steps across the line of scrimmage or steps to his outside, the quarterback keeps the ball on the keeper play. This is referred to as the

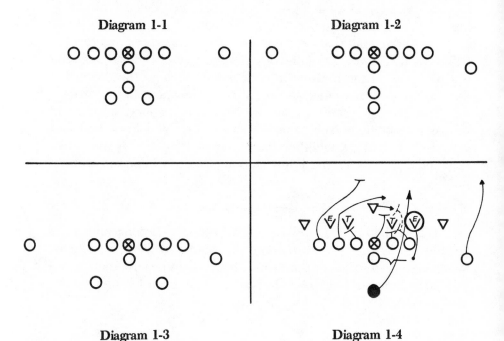

Diagram 1-1   Diagram 1-2

Diagram 1-3   Diagram 1-4

second option. (Diagrams 1-8, 1-9, and 1-10.) This is the quarterback's keeper play.

If the squared defender attacks the quarterback, the quarterback is coached to pitch the ball to the trailing back. (Diagrams 1-11, 1-12 and 1-13.) This is called the third option. Put these plays together and you have the Triple Option Series as described and diagrammed in the Wishbone, "I," and Pro Veer formations.

The primary objective of the Triple Option play is to isolate the first (dive) key, and also, to attack the second (keeper-pitch) key.

The first key is the first defender who shows outside of the offensive tackle's block (circled). If the first key steps across the line of scrimmage and does not attack the dive back, the quarterback is coached to hand the ball off to the dive back. (Diagrams 1-4, 1-5, 1-6, and 1-7.) If the first key attacks the dive back, the quarterback is coached to keep the ball and search for the second defensive key.

The second defensive key is the first defender to show outside of

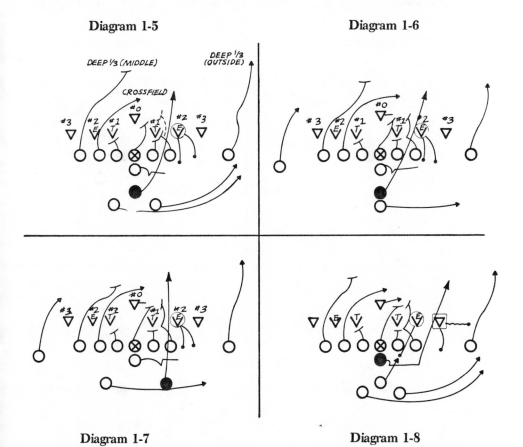

Diagram 1-5   Diagram 1-6

Diagram 1-7   Diagram 1-8

the first defensive key (squared). If the second defensive key feathers or shuffles to the outside to contain the potential pitch out or steps across the line of scrimmage to attack the pitchman, the quarterback is coached to keep the ball himself on a keeper play. (Diagrams 1-8, 1-9, and 1-10.) If the second defensive key attacks the quarterback, the ball handler is coached to pitch the ball to the trailing back. (Diagrams 1-11, 1-12, and 1-13.)

Whenever the second defensive key freezes on the line of scrimmage and does not attack the quarterback or the pitchman, the quarterback is coached to attack challenge the second defensive key. This means the quarterback should literally attack the second defensive key and force the defender to react to the quarterback or the pitchman. As soon as the quarterback challenges the second defensive key, he must be ready to keep the ball or pitch the ball quickly.

First (Dive) Key And Second (Pitch-Keep) Key Explanation

The eleven basic defenses we see during the fall are illustrated in the First (Dive) Key and Second (Pitch-Keep) Key Chart. Each de-

| Diagram 1-9 | Diagram 1-10 |

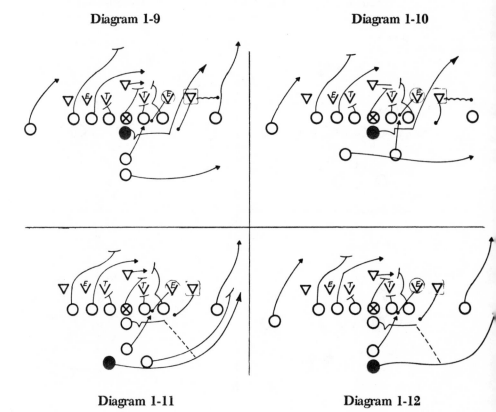

| Diagram 1-11 | Diagram 1-12 |

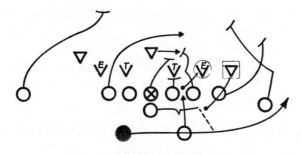

Diagram 1-13

fense is diagrammed and the potential first key (defender responsible for the dive back) is circled. The anticipated second key (defender responsible to tackle the quarterback) is squared. This is illustrated to both sides of the center. (Diagrams 1-14 to 1-23.)

A continual study of these eleven diagrams, combined with daily practice running against these defenses in dummie scrimmages, helps the quarterback to read his potential Triple Option keys prior to the snap of the ball.

After these keys have become second nature to the quarterback, the offensive staff explains the possible stunts where the defenders may exchange keys after the ball has been put into play. This is why we state, " . . . the first defender to show outside of the offensive tackle's block" or " . . . the first defender to show outside of the first defender."

Usually the chances are much greater for stunts to the split end's side because the linebacker is often off the line in a good blitzing position. (See Diagram 1-11.) Running the Triple Option to the tight end's side, it is much more difficult for the first and second keys to stunt or exchange defensive keys with one another. (Diagrams 1-14 to 1-22.) In Diagrams 1-23 and 1-24 the end and linebacker are in excellent positions to stunt or exchange defensive keys because of their stacked or almost stacked positions.

Numbering The Defensive Linemen And Linebackers

The defensive linemen and linebackers are given numbers to make the offensive blocking assignments brief and easier to understand.

Any defensive lineman or linebacker who lines head up on the center is the #0 man. Each lineman or linebacker from the center out is numbered consecutively 1 - 2 - 3 - 4. (Diagrams 1-25 through 1-35.)

One lineman lined up in the guard-center gap is #0 (Diagram

1-25); but, if there are two defenders in both gaps, each man is numbered #1 (Diagram 1-26).

Whenever there are stacked defenders lined up on an offensive lineman or in a gap, the near defender (lineman) is given the lowest number and the stacked linebacker is awarded the higher number. (Diagrams 1-31 and 1-35.)

FIRST (DIVE) KEY AND SECOND (PITCH-KEEP) KEY CHART

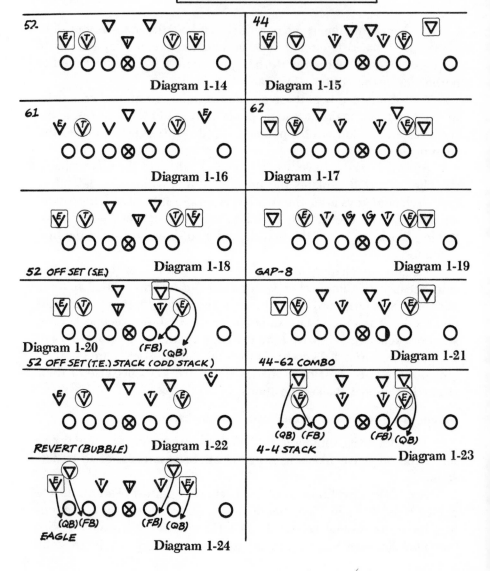

FIRST (DIVE) KEY = CIRCLE ○
SECOND (PITCH-KEEP) KEY = SQUARE □

Diagram 1-14

Diagram 1-15

Diagram 1-16

Diagram 1-17

52 OFF SET (S.E.)   Diagram 1-18

GAP-8   Diagram 1-19

Diagram 1-20   (FB) (QB)
52 OFF SET (T.E.) STACK (ODD STACK)

44-62 COMBO   Diagram 1-21

REVERT (BUBBLE)   Diagram 1-22

4-4 STACK   Diagram 1-23
(QB) (FB)   (FB) (QB)

(QB)(FB)   (FB) (QB)
EAGLE

Diagram 1-24

Triple Option Blocking Assignments

Split End	= Run off and block deep outside 1/3 area
Frontside Tackle	= Inside, Linebacker
Frontside Guard	= #1
Center	= #0 Frontside, Backside
Backside Guard	= #1

NUMBERING THE DEFENSIVE LINEMEN AND LINEBACKERS

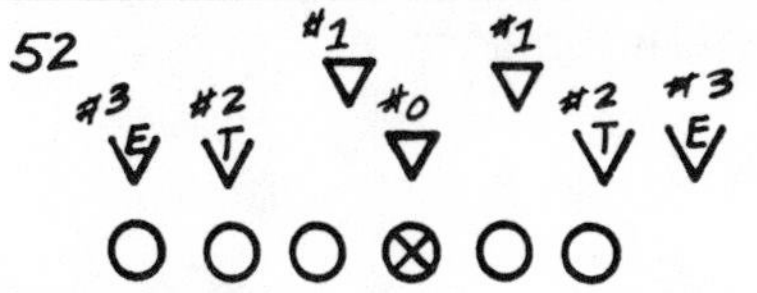

52

Diagram 1-25

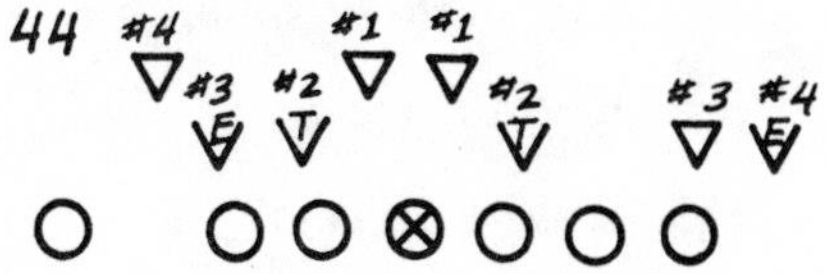

44

Diagram 1-26

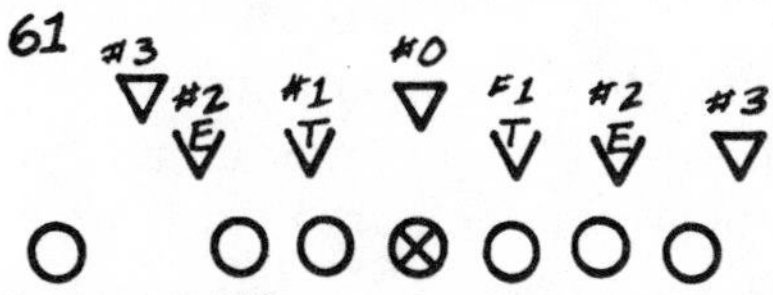

61

Diagram 1-27

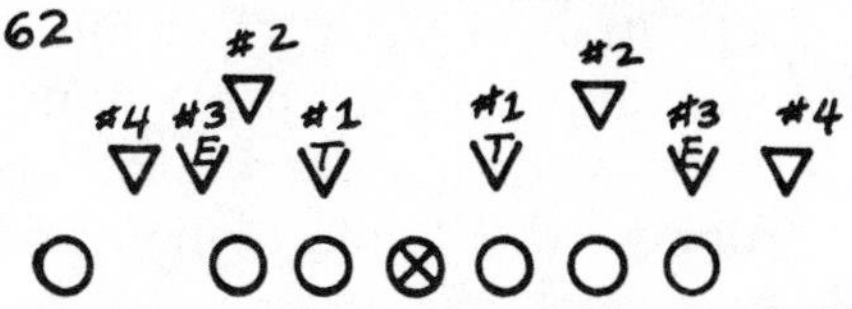

62

Diagram 1-28

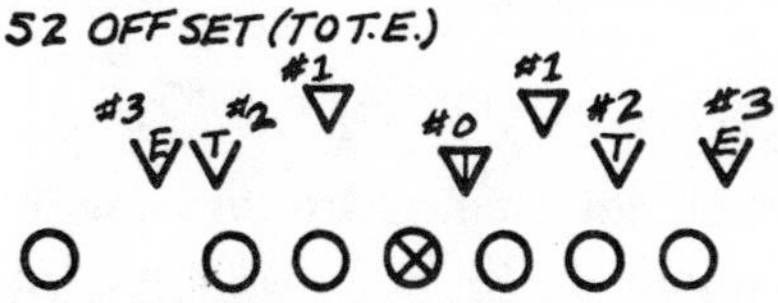

52 OFFSET (TO T.E.)

Diagram 1-29

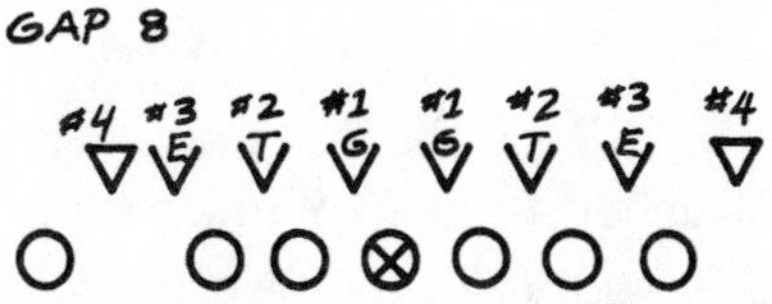

GAP 8

Diagram 1-30

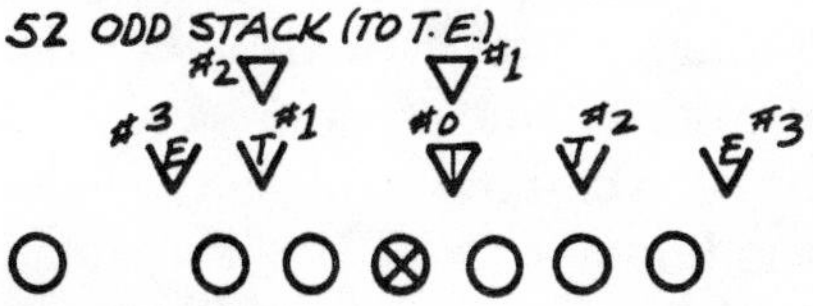

52 ODD STACK (TO T.E.)

Diagram 1-31

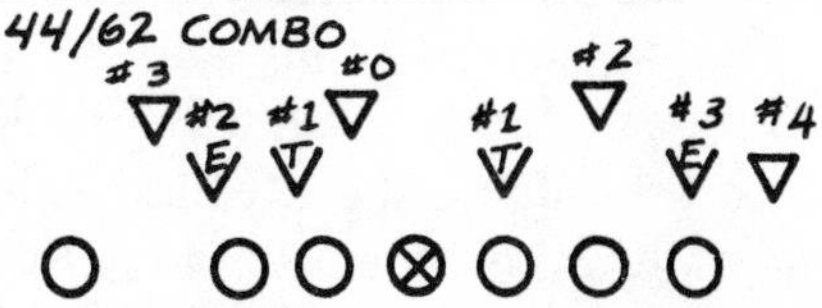

44/62 COMBO

Diagram 1-32

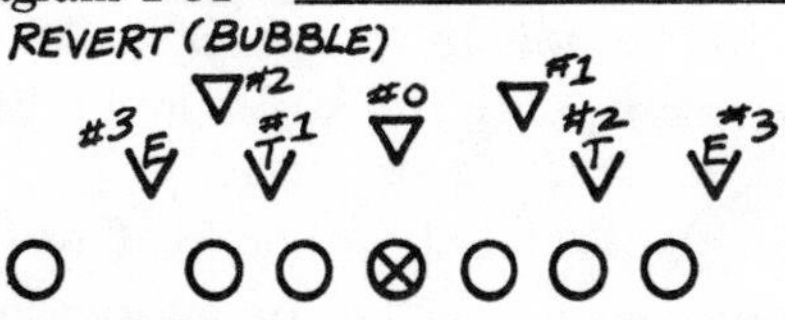

REVERT (BUBBLE)

Diagram 1-33

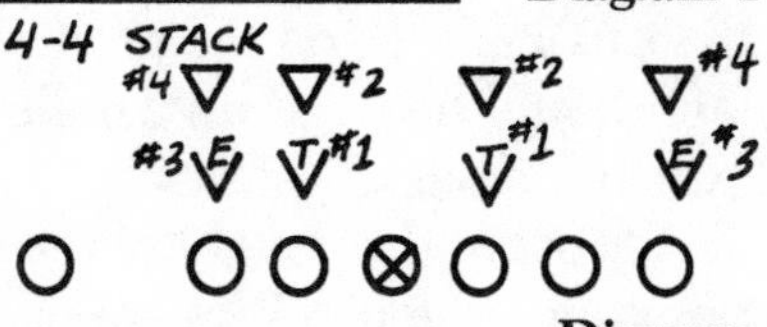

4-4 STACK

Diagram 1-34

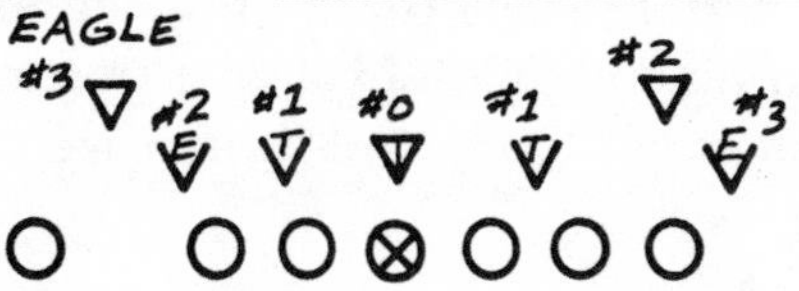

EAGLE

Diagram 1-35

| Backside Tackle | = Cut off #2 Crossfield to front of point of attack |
| Backside End | = Deep backside 1/3 area |

The above blocking assignments are illustrated in Diagrams 1-5, 1-6, and 1-7.

The offensive backfield assignments are as follows:

Quarterback	= Give, Pitchout, Keeper
Dive Back	= Dive
Pitchman	= Pitchout
(Leadback-Wishbone)	= Block Contain Man

(See Diagram 1-4.)

Triple Option Success

The success of the Triple Option play depends upon continual repetition of the correct fundamentals of offensive execution. The coaching staff must pay continual attention to the most minute detail of the techniques and fundamentals of all eleven offensive members running the Triple Option play. The overall simplicity of this play helps each offensive player out-execute the opposition's defenders.

Line Stance

All of the linemen, with the exception of the split end, are coached to line up in a four point stance. Both hands are down with the finger tips parallel to the line of scrimmage. Both hands should be in line with the offensive lineman's knees. The knees should be bent at a 45 degree angle, and the legs should be placed well under the lineman's body so he will be able to fire off the line of scrimmage. The butt should be slightly higher than the head and the head should be in a natural position. We do not want the linemen to lift the head in an unnatural or uncomfortable position. We coach the potential lineman to focus his eyes on the ground three to four feet in front of him. The feet should be lined up parallel to the hands, with the knees lined up over the ankles.

Most of the weight of the lineman should be placed on his finger tips, since the blockers are usually firing out forward or on a forward angle. Whenever we ask a lineman to pull, use a reach, or a cut off block, we teach the blocker to lessen his weight on his finger tips so he can move quickly on a parallel course to the line of scrimmage.

Two Foot Line Split Consistency

There is an inconsistency among Triple Option coaches pertaining to whether the two foot split between the center-guard and the guard-tackle should be constant. The consistency of the two foot split gives the fullback a constant course on all of his Triple Option dives so that many coaches favor this coaching point.

Other coaches like to increase the split between the guard-tackle gap to three and possibly four feet. Their reasoning is to make the defender cover more defensive area and give the blocking linemen, at the point of the attack, better blocking angles on the defenders.

Both of these coaching points have merit, but we begin with consistent two foot splits and only adjust the guard-tackle split later in the season. Our number one offensive objective is to minimize our offensive fumbles. Therefore, we prescribe beginning the season with a two foot line split from offensive tackle to tackle. The consistent two foot split assures the dive back a constant course to the crease area. This course insures a consistent quarterback-dive back mesh which minimizes Triple Option fumbles.

Why The Offensive Line Lines Up Off The Ball

Since the Triple Option running attack is based on a combination of option running and discriminating blocking, the offensive line lines up one foot off the ball. The coaching point behind lining up the offensive linemen as far off the ball as possible is to allow the blocking linemen a greater chance to read the defensive linemen's charge. It also gives the offensive linemen more time to get into the proper blocking lanes to execute their Triple Option blocking patterns. If the defense decides to game or stunt, it affords the offense more time to pick up these stunting techniques.

Numbering Defenders from Outside-In for Triple Option (Diagrams 4-6, 4-7, 4-8 & 4-9)

The defenders are numbered from the outside-in to designate specific defenders, using a simple numbering system rather than calling the defenders by position.

The outside-in numbering technique is used primarily for the perimeter defenders. This technique is a most helpful coaching method in explaining the Triple Option strategy to the quarterback, and perimeter blocking assignments to the lead blockers and wide-set offensive personnel. When calling the defenders by position, there is often a problem in semantics pertaining to whether the defender is an end or a tackle. Some coaches call specific defenders ends because they are on the end of the line of scrimmage or linebackers because they are linebackers in other defensive set ups. The Pro 40 or 61 Defense is an example of this personnel confusion among many coaches and players. (Diagram 1-36.)

Some players and coaches refer to the #3 defender to the tight end's side as an end because he is on the end of the line of scrimmage. Other staff members or players refer to the #3 defender as the linebacker because he plays linebacker in other defenses.

Therefore, the numbering from the outside-in read specifies the particular defender the coaching staff or squad member is talking about.

Sometimes the defenders to the split end's side may stunt and exchange positions as illustrated in Diagram 1-37. Again, we refer to these players by numbers rather than confusing fellow staff members or players by referring to these defenders by their pre-snap or post stunt positions.

The reason the outside corner back is given a 1 number to the split end side and a 2 number to the tight end side is the cornerman to the split side usually covers the deep outside 1/3 deep zone. (Diagram 1-38.) When the Triple Option is directed to the tight end side, the safetyman (1 man) usually is assigned to take the deep outside one-third area, while the corner back (2 man) levels off and plays the flat. (Diagram 1-39.)

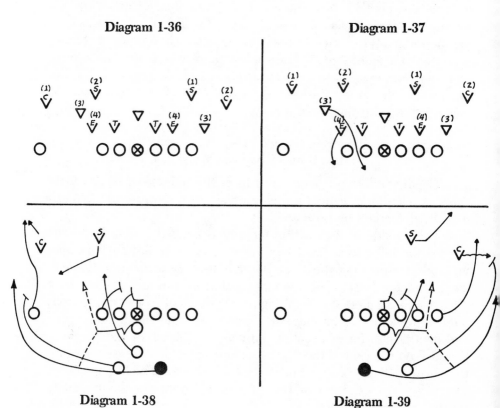

Diagram 1-36   **Diagram 1-37**

Diagram 1-38   **Diagram 1-39**

CHAPTER TWO

The Wishbone: Featuring Raw Power, Break Away, and Passing Threats

                            The Wishbone Formation derives its name from the backfield set which resembles a wishbone, with the fullback aligned closer to the line of scrimmage than the two offensive halfbacks. (Diagram 2-1.)

The Wishbone offensive formation is favored by many coaching staffs for the following reasons:

The most consistent maneuver to the split end's side is the Triple Option. Over the past ten years we have been searching for a sound play series that we could run, not only to the split side, but also to the tight end side. The mirrored success of this play has produced a consistent ground game against all of today's modern defenses. This balanced or mirrored attack affords each halfback the chance to com-

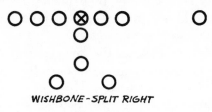

WISHBONE - SPLIT RIGHT

Diagram 2-1

plement one another. Since each halfback must block for one another, this competition situation makes each individual back a more consistent blocker.

The basic Triple Option play can strike with speed or power all along the defensive front. The actual point of the attack does not have to be determined until the defense has actually committed itself.

The simplicity of the Triple Option attack from the Wishbone formation is evident when one considers that 70 percent of all the plays called are the basic Triple Option plays; therefore, 70 percent of the practice planning sessions must be spent on this basic plan of attack.

The four back offense can be used effectively all over the field, especially from the offense's goal line to their twenty yard line and from the opposition's ten yard line to the opponent's goal line.

The offense mu.t split at least one receiver (split end) to maintain a successful passing attack. This wide threat also has the ability to drive one deep back backward and is responsible for the deep outside one third area.

The Triple Option from the Wishbone formation designates only one man (fullback) as the hand off man on the entire Triple Option series. Thus, only one man is responsible to set the first course through the crease instead of using one of two split backs to fake off to the Houston Triple Option series.

All four of the backs have an equal chance of carrying the ball. Therefore there is no chance of running a one back offense as used in many "I"-like formations. In the Wishbone attack, the quarterback gives the ball to the runner which the defense leaves uncovered or free.

The Triple Option series forces the defense to assign a defender to one of the three points of the attack along the line of scrimmage. These three assigned defenders are responsible for each potential ball carrier, whether he has the ball or has a chance to carry the ball. Thus, this play cuts down to the defensive pursuit action. Therefore the three points along the line, plus the end taking the deep defender to the deep outside one third area, ties up at least four defenders to each side of the line of scrimmage.

The Wishbone attack has the raw power to run over the defense, along with the break away threat of both the running backs and the quick bomb to the split receiver. Thus the Wishbone attack has the flexibility to run a balanced offensive attack combining passing, break away running, and power.

The minimum number of plays used are consistent week to week, regardless of the type of defensive strategy the opposition sets up. The Triple Option, counter option, halfback counter, and inside belly plays are the four basic plays in our series. The combination of simplicity and consistency of the Triple Option attack makes coaching this system a pleasure.

The long gainer ability of the Triple Option running attack often minimizes the importance of the pass. This means, if on third down and eight yards to go the opposition sets their defense to stop the expected pass, the Triple Option running attack has a high percentage chance of exploding for the first down, or, with offensive speed in the backfield, a chance to break the long touchdown run.

The Triple Option attack forces the defense to use a balanced attack. If the opposition loads the defense to stop an anticipated play to the wide side of the field or to the tight end side, the offense may break away a long gainer to the opposite side of the opponent's defense.

A well trained offensive field general may be coached to successfully read the defensive strategy, so he is able to automatically read the defense after the ball has been put into play. This means the quarterback does not have to use an elaborate automatic play calling system just prior to the snap of the ball, but is able to read the defensive strategy *now* while the play is actually in progress.

The quarterback's Triple Option read after the ball has been put into play minimizes the effectiveness of the defensive stunting and gaming strategy. This means that the defense may blitz, game or stunt, but with the proper read by the quarterback, all the stunts and games actually hurt the defense. The quarterback is coached to believe in a philosophy that the opposition weakens itself whenever it has to attack the Wishbone with blitzes and games, because it changes the defender's routine assignment of attacking on the option. During gaming and blitzing calls, the defender is forced to move and think at the same time which cuts down the defender's instinctive defensive ability.

We believe the Triple Option offensive attack has a greater advantage over the defense, because we have run our attack every day for several years, while the opposition's defense may only have three to four days to prepare for our offense.

The Triple Option can be run from two wide receivers to either side (split end to one side and a flanker back to the opposite side, or a split end to the left and the right) or with two wide receivers to one side (flanker back and split end both on the same side of the line). While breaking the three back Wishbone alignment elminates the lead back's block, the flanker back's wide alignment places new pressure on the defense's perimeter alignment.

The Triple Option has the flexibility of a quick hitter (fullback dive), the delayed keep (quarterback keep), and the wide threat (half-back pitch sweep). Each time the Triple Option is called, the pressure is placed upon the defense because the quarterback is coached to take any one of these three plays (to one side of the line of scrimmage) which the defense gives up.

Since a balanced defense must assign a defender to take the (1) fullback, (2) quarterback, (3) pitch, (4) deep one third area to both sides of the line of scrimmage, the defense has only three men to defend the middle of the defense. It is therefore our philosophy, if we want to block the defender who is responsible for the fullback, and we can successfully run the fullback dive or cut play with great consistency.

With the exception of flip-flopping the tight end and the split end, all the other nine offensive players line up in their normal alignment in basic Wishbone formation. This means we do not have to adjust our nine offensive players' stance, path, or blocking techniques.

The threat of the long pass is a constant weapon because at least one wide receiver releases off the line of scrimmage on each option play. This forces the defensive secondary to respect the pass and aids the running attack.

The ball carrier has the quick chance to run to daylight because the Triple Option faking takes place on the line of scrimmage rather than deep in the offensive backfield.

The line blocking rules are easy to execute, and these blockers have excellent blocking angles on the defenders because only the interior defenders, inside of the offensive tackles, must be blocked. Thus, the interior offensive line screens or seals off the defensive inside pursuit so smooth execution by the quarterback allows the ball carrier a solid chance to turn the corner for the long gainer.

CHAPTER THREE

How To Coach The
Triple Option Quarterback

Quarterback's Stance and Alignment

The quarterback should line up in a parallel stance with the feet lined up below the ball handler's armpits. The quarterback's knees should be bent slightly in a relaxed stance. The quarterback's right hand should be placed in the center's crotch, slightly deeper than his wrists. The thumbs of both hands should be placed slightly forward so that the joint of the right thumb fits into the left hand thumb's groove, just below the first point. The top hand should exert upward pressure on the center's butt so the center will have a specific target to aim the ball.

The shoulders should be relaxed and the quarterback's elbows should be bent slightly. The bend in the elbows is important so that the quarterback is able to ride the center forward as the center fires out to block the assigned defender.

Just as the ball strikes the quarterback's top hand, the quarterback should begin to kick back with the foot to the playside. This foot should step backward, reaching the fullback as soon as possible. The quarterback's elbows must be kept close to the body.

The moment the quarterback receives the ball from the center, he is coached to pull the ball into his "third hand" in order to protect the ball and make his ball handling more deceptive.* The ball handler must keep his body between the ball and the defenders to protect the ball and to be a more effective faker.

---

*Some coaches teach the quarterback to take the ball from the center and thrust it immediately toward the first key and not pull the ball into the third hand.

Quarterback's Directional Step and Read

As the ball is snapped into the quarterback's hands, the ball handler is coached to focus his eyes on his first defensive key (circled in Diagram 3-1). The first defensive key is the first defender to show outside of the playside offensive tackle. This means the quarterback must use his peripheral vision to pick up the expected defender prior to the snap of the ball. Once the ball has been put into play, the quarterback looks directly at his first defensive key (circled in Diagram 3-1) and uses peripheral vision to see the fullback's pocket. The quarterback's use of peripheral vision and kinesthetic awareness must be acquired through continual practice in pre-practice and post practice, as well as daily practice sessions. The ball handler must keep the ball parallel to the ground.

The quarterback must make a quick mental check of the defense to check the outside forcing units to both sides of the line of scrimmage. If the quarterback looks only to the side of scrimmage the ball is directed, the defense will be able to zero into on a particular side of the line of scrimmage. The quarterback should line up in a comfortable balanced stance with his weight on the balls of his feet. His first step should be a short step on a 45 degree angle with the right foot aimed at five o'clock. (Diagram 3-2.)

Quarterback's First Step

The quarterback is coached to take 45 degree step backward with his right foot (running the Triple Option right). The quarterback should extend his arms back and reach the fullback as deep as possible on the ball handler's first step. (Diagrams 3-3 and 3-4.)

As soon as the first step hits the ground, the quarterback is coached to fully extend his arms and place the ball into the fullback's pocket, while keeping his eyes on his first key. The ball must be placed firmly into the fullback's pocket. The right hand must be placed on one side of the ball and directly between the ball and the fullback's stomach. The coaching point behind this ball placement is to allow the quarterback's back hand the possibility to place pressure against the fullback's stomach—to allow the quarterback room to pull out the football if the fullback mistakenly attempts to clamp down upon the ball. The quarterback then takes an adjustment step with his left foot and is coached to never ride the ball beyond his belt buckle.

Quarterback' Second Step

The second step is a drag-like step with the left foot which is used as a balanced step to allow the quarterback to make a short ride to the fullback. The second step also keeps him off the line of scrimmage and

Diagram 3-1 **Diagram 3-2**

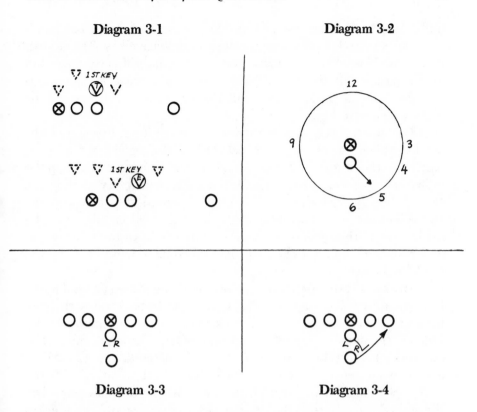

Diagram 3-3 **Diagram 3-4**

enables the ball handler a straight path to work parallel to the line of scrimmage. The quarterback makes this second adjustment step as he rides the ball to the fullback. Since the fullback is running at a 45 degree angle away from the quarterback, the ball handler must not ride the fullback beyond his second step, or a fumble may result from the quarterback overextending himself. Therefore, if the quarterback decides to give the ball to the fullback, he must do so before the second step hits the ground to insure a perfect mesh. (Diagram 3-5.)

Adjustment Step

The length of the adjustment step depends upon the speed of the fullback. This adjustment step is necessary to continue to ride the

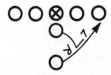

Diagram 3-5

fullback up to the quarterback's buckle (midline), while the ball hand-ler is coached to keep his eyes on the first defensive key. This adjust-ment step should not be made towards the line of scrimmage but rather parallel to the line of scrimmage. He must maintain this straight, parallel option path until the ball handler challenges the second defensive key.

The quarterback must not stride too far out in his first step, or he will force the fullback off his correct course. The second step must be parallel to the first step. If the second step is too long, it may trip the fullback; therefore, it is the quarterback's responsibility to slide the second step back slightly if he feels the second step may trip the inside foot of the fullback. Another reason the ball handler must be ready to slide the second foot back slightly is to give the fullback the opportunity to cut back close to a possible double team block by the tackle and guard.

The second step (left adjustment) should be placed parallel to the lead (right) step. (Diagram 3-5.) If the quarterback rides the ball beyond his belt buckle, the fullback may cut off the quarterback's vision of the first key and will throw off the Triple Option timing. The quarterback must keep the ball in continual motion but must be careful not to rush the fullback ride, because it will throw off the timing of the fullback's path. This may allow the defensive first key the ability to easily read the quarterback-fullback's mesh, and makes it impossible for the quarterback to fully extend his arms while riding the fullback. The quarterback must be coached to stay parallel to the line of scrimmage and must never fade deeper than his parallel path. The path must always be parallel to the line of scrimmage.

Eliminate False Step

To eliminate the quarterback's false step, we teach the ball hand-ler to dig his toes into the ground. This actually makes the quarter-back put his weight on his toes and this eliminates the unnecessary sliding or false stepping by the quarterback. Since the speed and execution by the quarterback must be perfected, a false step by the ball handler could throw off the entire timing of the play and may result in a fumble or missed assignment.

First Key (Dive Key)

If the first key (first man outside of the offensive tackle) does not attack the fullback and attacks the quarterback, the quarterback leaves the ball in the fullback's pocket and continues down the line carrying out his Triple Option fake. (Diagram 3-6.)

As soon as the fullback accepts the ball, he should slap his elbow with the lower hand of his pocket. This locks the football firmly in place inside of the fullback's pocket.

If the first key (first man outside of the offensive tackle) attacks the fullback, the quarterback is taught to pull out the ball and continue along his parallel to the line of scrimmage path and challenge the second defensive key. (Diagram 3-7.)

Second Key (Pitch-Keeper Key)

The quarterback is coached to challenge the second key (first defensive man to show outside of the first defensive key). When challenging the second key, the ball handler should keep his shoulders parallel to the sidelines. If the second key feathers (shuffles) away from the quarterback, the ball handler is coached to keep the ball. He should plant the back foot and explode straight ahead across the line of scrimmage, running in a north or south direction. The quarterback should drop the inside shoulder and run low and hard like a fullback, and expect to be hit from the inside by the defensive pursuit. (Diagram 3-8.)

If the second defensive key attacks the quarterback, the ball handler must be ready to make a soft pitch to the left halfback. The pitch should be made with a loose wrist and the near side foot should point directly at the potential ball carrier. The pitch should be soft with a slow end over end roll. The quarterback should extend his arm

Diagram 3-6

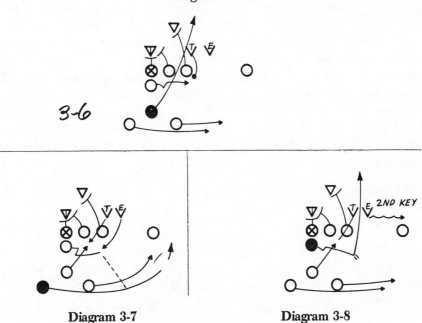

Diagram 3-7   Diagram 3-8

from the elbow with the fingers of the pitch hand pointing upward. The quarterback steps with the same foot he pitches the ball with. In the Triple Option right, the quarterback makes his pitch with his right hand as he steps with his right foot toward the pitch man (left halfback). (Diagram 3-9.)

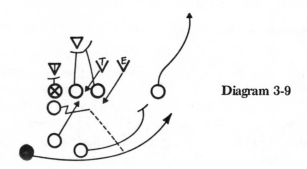

Diagram 3-9

We instruct our quarterback to try and make the pitch and only keep the ball on an obvious keeper play. The field general must stay on a straight line and not fade off the line toward the pitchman. The only time the quarterback is coached to step backward is to avoid penetration by a defensive lineman, after the quarterback has made his fake and is about to challenge the second key.

Quarterback's Eyes

On the snap of the ball, the quarterback is coached to focus his eyes on the first defender (who shows) outside of the offensive tackle's block. This is the quarterback's first read. The quarterback is taught to read this defender picking up the dive man with peripheral vision because the diving fullback always runs the same course regardless of the opposition's defense. The quarterback must keep his eyes on the first key as he places the ball into the dive man's pocket, because the action of this defender tells the quarterback whether to hand the ball off or pull the ball out of the pocket and challenge the second defensive key.

Eye Control

The quarterback's eyes control all of his hand and feet movements along the line of scrimmage. The quarterback is responsible to fasten his eyes on his first key. He must pick up the dive back's pocket area with peripheral vision. He must then focus his eyes on the second defender to option and must keep the trail man in sight using peripheral vision.

As soon as the quarterback keeps the ball, he must read the flow of the defense to determine whether he should drive straight ahead for three and one half yards or cut to his inside or outside; thus, the quarterback must have quick eyes as well as quick hands and feet.

Ball Handling

The quarterback keeps both hands on the ball and pitches the ball with one hand just at the very last moment. The ball should never stop moving during the full operation of the Triple Option. The ride to the fullback is actually a smooth flowing motion. The ball should be carried parallel to the ground, and it should be pointed directly at the first defensive key just before the quarterback puts the ball into the fullback's pocket. The head, eyes, and feet should be coordinated with the flowing fake to the fullback.

Practice putting the ball on the far hip of the fullback when running the Triple Option. This forces the quarterback to fully extend his arms on his quick give or ride fake to the fullback. Placing the ball on the fullback's far hip helps to freeze the defenders. This freeze or hold on the interior as well as the perimeter defenders is responsible for making the second and third segments of the Triple Option successful.

First Point of Decision

The first point of decision is made by the quarterback as he rides the fullback toward the line of scrimmage. As soon as the quarterback puts the ball into the fullback's pocket, the ball handler is able to focus his complete attention upon the first defender outside of the offensive tackle's block. During this time, the quarterback may give the ball to the fullback if the first key does not attack the fullback. If the defender attacks the fullback, the quarterback pulls the ball out of the fullback's pocket and keeps the ball. The field general continues along his straight path and looks for the second defensive key.

Second Point of Decision

The second point of decision is the next defender to show outside of the first defensive key. The quarterback is coached to attempt to get the pitch off first and to keep the ball only in an obvious situation. This obvious situation is whenever the second defensive key attempts to defend against the pitchman (left halfback). Thus, the quarterback becomes an automatic ball carrier by keeping the ball and cutting upfield inside of the second defensive key. If the second key attacks the quarterback, the ball handler is coached to make the pitch out to the trailing back. If the second defensive key hangs on the line of scrimmage, the quarterback is taught to challenge the defender by running directly at the defender and making the second key attack the quarterback. The ball handler must make up his mind quickly and be ready to pitch or keep quickly.

Quarterback's Ride Fake

The quarterback is coached to never ride the fullback beyond the ball handler's belt buckle. Actually, we teach the quarterback to ride the fullback from the dive man's pocket to the quarterback's near hip. The quarterback should reach back and place the ball in the fullback's pocket as soon as possible. This allows the quarterback more time to watch the first defensive key. The reason most quarterbacks have trouble reading the first key is because they don't step far enough backward on the lead step and begin to ride the fullback too late. This short riding technique also gives the quarterback too brief a view of the first defensive key. If the quarterback rides the fullback past the ball handler's belt buckle, he will ruin the timing of the Triple Option play. Riding the ball past the quarterback's body midline gives the first defensive key more of a chance to tackle the fullback, quarterback, or both offensive backs at the same time.

The fullback's pocket should never interfere with the quarterback's ride because the fullback is coached to take the ball softly only with the bottom arm. The fullback must stay on his designated course toward the offensive crease. He is taught to never cut back or adjust his course until the quarterback actually gives the dive man the ball or pulls the ball out to attack the second defensive key.

During the entire ride, the quarterback's shoulders should be parallel to the sidelines, and the ball handler should always handle the ball at the level of his belt buckle.

The quarterback's decision is based upon the defensive first key and his decision step is the second foot. This means the quarterback hands the ball off or pulls the ball out by the time his adjustment (second step) is made.

The mesh between the quarterback-fullback must be perfected before time is spent working on the problems of attacking the second key. This means the quarterback must accomplish the first phase of the Triple Option before he is able to move on to the second option phase.

Faking Quarterback

The ball handler should never overfake. He should make it look like he has the ball after handing the ball off. The faker should keep his body between the defender and the fake. The field general is coached to never follow the ball carrier with his eyes, but to continue through with his faking. Prior to the quarterback's first read, the quarterback points the ball directly at the first defender outside of the offensive tackle. Once the quarterback places the ball into the fullback's pocket, the guessing defender is frozen because he does not know whether the quarterback will hand the ball off to the fullback or keep the ball. Since the quarterback is reading this defender, the defensive man is wrong whether he decides to attack the fullback (quarterback keeps the ball) or steps out to attack the quarterback (quarterback hands the ball off to the fullback).

Once the quarterback decides to run the keeper, he is taught to curl his body over the ball, drop the inside shoulder, hold the ball in both hands with each hand over the point of the ball, and ram straight ahead with power.

Altering the Collision Path

The ball handler may have to alter his parallel path slightly off the line if the first defensive key penetrates and tackles the lineman deep enough to force the quarterback to step around this collision. If this happens, the ball handler is coached to get back on his parallel path as soon as possible so he can challenge the second defensive key and maintain his four by four yard ratio with the trailing pitchman.

The Quarterback Keeper

The only time the quarterback is taught to keep the ball is when the second defensive key feathers or shuffles away from the quarterback or steps across the line of scrimmage to play the the pitchman all the way.

The Keeper Technique

As soon as the quarterback decides to keep the ball, he is coached to pull the ball out of the fullback's pocket, plant and push off the back foot, dip the inside shoulder, and cover the football with both hands. The ball should be cradled in the inside hand and covered over the top by the outside hand. Both hands on the ball protects the ball from being pulled out by a defender's arm tackle or popped out by a solid hit from a blind side tackler. When in traffic, the ball carrier must keep the ball in both hands, tucked firmly in his third hand (stomach). It is only when the quarterback breaks free that he is taught to run with the ball in one hand.

If In Doubt, Keep The Ball

Our quarterback is coached to keep the ball and not pitch out if he has any second thoughts. This means we want our quarterback to get off the pitch first and foremost whenever possible. But if the defense is using a particular stunt or technique which confuses our quarterback versus the second key, we tell our quarterback to keep the ball and drive for his three and one half yards. One bad pitch out minimizes ten good pitch outs.

Keep The Ball Versus A #4 Technique Defender

If the first key is lined up in a #4 technique (defender is lined up over the playside tackle's nose), the quarterback should think "keep the ball," after riding the fullback, and option the next defender. (Diagram 3-10.) The #4 defender is coached to close down as soon as the offensive tackle blocks down and crosses his face.

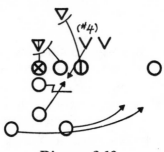

Diagram 3-10

The first key aligned in a #4 technique is the most difficult first key read for the quarterback. Therefore, we emphasize pulling the ball out of the fullback's pocket and attacking, the second defensive key. Now the quarterback has more time to read the second key, and he can keep the ball or pitch the ball, depending upon the reactions of the outside key.

Coaching Point: Perhaps the words "Pull the ball out of the fullback's pocket" would be better than "Keep the ball," versus the defender in a #4 technique. By "*keeping* the ball," the author means for the quarterback to keep the ball and attack the second defensive key.

Ball Adjustment Prior To The Pitch

Just prior to challenging the second defensive key, the quarterback is coached to move the ball with two hands from his third hand (stomach) upward to his chest. There are two reasons why the quarterback is taught to make the pitch from the chest: First, there is less wasted motion and less chance of a wild pitch when it is made from the chest. The pitch should be made with a loose wrist and the pitch then becomes only a slight extension from the right elbow. This pitch should resemble a basketball jump shot technique. Second, we coach the quarterback to pitch from a higher position than his stomach, so if the defender tackles the quarterback high, the chest pass is better equipped to break the defender's bear high-like grip. If the defender tackles the quarterback around the waist, the quarterback is able to make the pitch with little effort.

Pitch Out First, Keep Only When Forced

The quarterback should always think, "pitch." The only time the quarterback is coached to keep the ball on a Triple Option is when the defense definitely takes away the pitch out; thus, the quarterback is taught to make the pitch on the second defensive key. The option of the keep is forced upon the ball handler by the defense.

Quarterback's Pitch Out

The pitch out is made by the quarterback with one arm. The outside arm is extended, and the ball is pitched with a loose wrist to make sure the flight of the ball is a dead or knuckle ball floating action. The pitch should be passed in a firm, flat trajectory. We coach the quarterback and the trailing halfback to work for a four-four relationship. This means the pitchman should be four yards outside and four yards deeper than the pitching quarterback. (Diagram 3-11.)

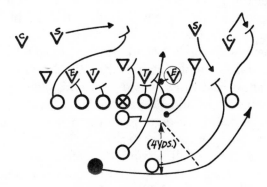

Diagram 3-11

Timing The Pitch Out

The timing of the pitch out between the quarterback and the pitchman must be constant on all plays. As soon as the quarterback decides to keep the ball after faking to the dive man, the quarterback should challenge the second defender. If the second key attacks the quarterback, the ball handler should make a quick end-over-end knuckle ball-like pitch to the pitchman. The quarterback is instructed to pick up the pitchman with his eyes just before the ball leaves his pitching hand. The ball handler must step toward the pitch out target with the same foot, same hand, as the quarterback makes the pitch out.

The Quick Triple Option Pitch

The quarterback must be ready to make a quick pitch out to the trailing halfback as soon as he fakes the ball to the fullback. This is particularly true if the quarterback is an outstanding runner. The defensive strategy behind forcing or crashing the second key is to take away the strong running threat of the quarterback and force the ball handler to pitch the ball to a less explosive running back. Therefore, the quick pitch out must be continually practiced in daily practice sessions. Since we do not want the quarterback to be hit live in all of these sessions, we give a defender an air dummy, and he uses this shield to explode into the quarterback's face as soon as the fullback passes the quarterback.

Left Handed Pitch

When the Triple Option is run to the offensive left side, the quarterback makes a left handed pitch. The ball is still held in two hands after the short ride to the fullback, and then the quarterback adjusts the ball to his chest with both hands. As he looks directly at the second key, the first defender to show outside of the first key, the pitch is made with the left hand. The wrist should be kept loose and the pitch is made simply by extending the arm from the elbow. This one hand chest pass is a soft end-over-end pitch.

The left foot should be pointed directly at the pitchman. The reason the left hand is used to pitch the ball when running the Triple Option left is to keep the quarterback's body and right arm between the defender and the ball. Even if the defender tackles the ball hand-ler before or during the pitch, the quarterback can make a successful pitch. The left handed pitch for the right handed quarterback must be continually worked on to gain consistency. The pitch should be made with the fingers pointed upward and the pitch arm should follow through directly at the intended receiver. The quarterback's eyes should be trained on the target which is about a foot and one half to two feet in front of the pitchman. The amount of lead on the pitch depends upon the speed of the pitchman, his depth, and the distance between the quarterback and the target area. We feel that the perfect depth and lead is a four by four yard ratio. Of course this four by four yard relationship may be adjusted, if the potential ball carrier is faced to turn upfield inside of the lead halfback's kick out block. The quarterback must always make the pitch out above the pitchman's waist. The best pitch is usually about chest high. The quarterback's shoulders should always be parallel to the sidelines when the ball handler makes his pitch. Through our film study over the years, most poor pitches have been made when the quarterback has decided to keep the ball and then makes the pitch at the last moment when his shoulders are not parallel to the sidelines.

How To Pitch On The Run

The Triple Optioning quarterback must learn to pitch on the run. He must *not* make a habit of breaking down into a slow shuffle every time he wishes to make a pitch to the trailing back. Continual practice at sprinting and making the one hand pitch will make this technique second nature for the optioning quarterback. The optioning quarterback must be coached to soften the pitch with the increase in his own lateral speed, since there is a tendency for the ball handler to put too much speed on the pitch the faster he runs.

The quarterback must be ready to make a quicker pitch to the split end side than to the tight end side because the defender responsible for the ball handler is one man closer to the optioning quarterback. The young quarterback has the tendency to fire a rushed pitch.

How To Absorb The Blow After The Pitch

As soon as the pitch is made, the quarterback is coached to turn his shoulders from parallel to the sidelines to parallel to the line of scrimmage to absorb the outside-in tackle by the outside defender. We teach the quarterback to turn his back to the defender and to relax in a "fetal-like" bunched position.

After making the pitch, the quarterback is taught to relax and be ready to be hit by the defender who has been assigned to tackle the quarterback. We teach the quarterback to make a slight one quarter turn so that his back is turned directly opposite the outside defender who is attacking the quarterback from an outside-in position. If the defender is assigned to attack the quarterback from an inside-out position, the quarterback's back is automatically turned toward the defender.

The quarterback's outside arm may also be used to ward off or protect the ball from the outside defender.

Another method of protection the quarterback may use as a change of pace is to actually charge into the attacking outside defender with the inside shoulder and forearm after the pitch has been executed to the trailing halfback. This punishing, rolling action by the quarterback tends to take a lot of zip out of the surprised, crashing defender and helps to prevent injury to the exposed previous ball handler.

How To Read The Dive Key (Wishbone, "I", Veer)

The quarterback must be coached how to read the dive key before the center has snapped the ball. If the ball handler can read the first dive key (first defensive key) by alignment, he will have a predetermined idea of the first defender he must read. If the defender is aligned in a #4 defensive technique (head up), the quarterback must think "keep" (pull the ball out), and key the next defender outside of the #4 defender for the second read of the Triple Option attack. (Diagram 3-12.)

Diagram 3-12

The reason the quarterback is coached to keep the ball is the defensive tackle in a #4 defensive technique has the ability of closing down right now on the fullback. This quick closing technique is insured by the offensive tackle's inside blocking course, since the defensive tackle is coached to close down directly behind the blocking tackle's tail.

Coaching Point: All of the defenders have their defensive positions numbered by the offense, just as the defensive staff numbers the defenders for purposes of defensive alignment. This is discussed in Chapter 5.

If the defender is aligned in a 45 defensive technique (outside shoulder), the quarterback should first think "keep" (pull the ball out), unless this 45 defender steps to the outside or goes straight across the line of scrimmage. (Diagram 3-13.)

If the defender is aligned in a 7 defensive technique (in the gap outside of the offensive tackle), the quarterback should first think "give the ball to the dive man," unless the #7 defender closes down hard to a #5 technique. (Diagram 3-14.)

The reader will note that the quarterback is coached to give the ball to the fullback (Diagram 3-14) only when the defense "forces" the ball handler to give the dive man.

How To Read The Pitch Key

The pitch key is the first defender outside of the dive key. If the end man on the line of scrimmage (pitch key) holds or closes down toward the quarterback, the ball handler is coached to always pitch the ball to the trailing back. If the defensive end holds or closes to the inside, the quarterback does not have to challenge the end because the four by four yard pitch out relationship between the quarterback and the pitchman makes it impossible for the defensive end to take the proper defensive angle to cut off the ball carrier. (Diagram 3-15.) The only way the defensive end is able to get back to pursue the ball carrier correctly downfield is to retrace his steps and then sprint after the ball carrier.

The quarterback keeps the ball on the keeper play only when the end man on the line of scrimmage (pitch key) shuffles to the outside or drives straight across the line of scrimmage (straight upfield). (Diagram 3-16.)

Normally the end man on the line of scrimmage (pitch key) to the split end side begins to attack the quarterback as soon as he begins his

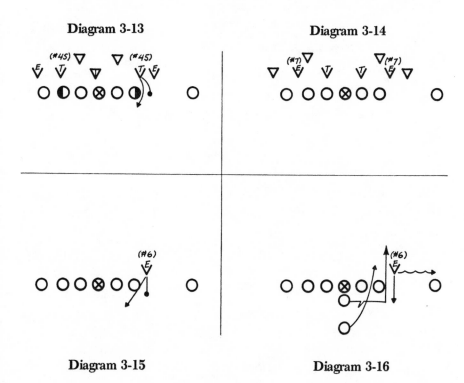

Diagram 3-13   Diagram 3-14

Diagram 3-15   Diagram 3-16

fullback hand off; therefore, the quarterback must be ready to pitch quickly when running the Triple Option to the split end's side of the offense. The quarterback should anticipate the quick pitch even more quickly to the split end side when running the two back "I" triple attack, because there is no threat of the lead back's block.

Therefore, the quarterback must be coached to make the pitch out at full speed on the run. If the quarterback begins to break down or brace himself before making the pitch out, the inside pursuit plus the end man on the line of scrimmage has a chance to recover from the dive fake and may tackle the pitchman for a loss or force a fumble on the pitch out maneuver.

CHAPTER FOUR

Wishbone's Triple Option
Backfield Techniques

Chapter 4 describes and illustrates the Wishbone's backfield fundamentals, assignments, and techniques. This chapter ties in with Chapter 3 pertaining to the offensive quarterback's Triple Option coaching points.

The Wishbone backfield must strive for perfection in execution to run the successful Triple Option play. There is only one method for perfecting execution and that is practicing the correct fundamentals and techniques described in this chapter.

Fullback's Stance and Depth

The fullback's heels should be 13 feet behind the front tip of the football. His alignment should be directly behind the quarterback's position. The fullback assumes a four point position, but with a more balanced stance than the four point offensive stance of the linemen. Therefore, he places less weight on his finger tips, because he will usually be taking off on a 45 degree angle or parallel to the line of scrimmage, depending upon the play called. The fullback's feet should be aligned in a parallel line so he can push off either foot for a quick start in any direction.

Unlike his offensive linemen's normal head position, the fullback is taught to keep his head up and his eyes forward so he can use peripheral vision, looking at the crease.

Fullback's Course

The fullback is coached to take a short six inch lead step, with the near foot, toward the outside hip of the playside offensive guard. This course should take the fullback on a 45 degree path, which should result in the fullback's inside shoulder just to the outside hip of the offensive guard's original position. The fullback's underarm should make a soft acceptance curl on the ball if the quarterback gives the ball to the dive man. If the quarterback decides to give the ball to the fullback, he is taught to make a soft fold with his pocket over the ball.

Once the fullback is given the ball, he is taught to key the playside tackle's block and break upfield off this block. The quarterback-fullback hand off (mesh) should begin on the fullback's second step.

The fullback is coached to use maximum speed when entering the crease. His speed must be constant, regardless whether he is the ball carrier, faker, or blocker. He must always be ready to be hit as he enters the crease area, because some defenses assign as many as three defenders on the fullback versus the Triple Option. (Diagram 4-1.)

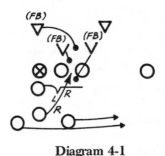

Diagram 4-1

As soon as the fullback approaches the hand off area, he is taught to form his pocket, lifting the inside elbow high and placing the outside hand on his belt buckle with the palm up. When the quarterback places the ball into the fullback's pocket, the inside should be back with the outside foot forward. The technique behind this coaching point is, as the quarterback steps toward the fullback, he may trip the fullback if the fullback's inside foot rips over the quarterback's lead foot. The other reason is, if the fullback's inside foot is stepping forward just as the quarterback makes the hand off, there is a chance that the fullback's inside knee may strike the football and pop the ball loose.

The fullback is coached to favor the double team block. This means that if the right offensive tackle double teams with the right offensive guard, the ball carrying fullback should set a path just outside of the double team block.

If the quarterback does not give the ball to the fullback, the fullback becomes an active blocker. This means the faker runs the same course, just outside of the crease, created by the tackle's block and looks for the first inside defender to show. Against the 52 defense, it is normally the playside inside Oklahoma linebacker. If no defender shows quickly from the inside, the fullback should continue his fake downfield and block the first off-colored jersey he finds.

The Crease

The Triple Option success is dependent upon a crease or lane which must be opened between the original position of the offensive guard and the offensive tackle. The guard and tackle's basic blocking rules, along with offensive blocking calls made at the line of scrimmage, will open up the Triple Option crease. The blocking calls on the line of scrimmage are necessary because different defenses predicate the offensive blockers' using different blocking angles and techniques. (Diagram 4-2.)

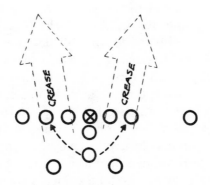

Diagram 4-2

Fullback's Pocket

When the quarterback actually gives the fullback the ball, he is taught to accept the ball with the lower hand. The fullback should not try to clamp down with the top arm. As soon as he accepts the ball, the fullback should hit the seam between his offensive guard and tackle and sprint through the offensive crease. The fullback is coached to change his path only when he arrives inside the guard-tackle's original gap.

Whenever the fullback does not get the ball, he should continue to fake through the crease, exactly like he has the ball, holding his left elbow with his right hand and his right elbow with his left hand. The fullback is taught to move the fake pocket back and forth just as if he were carrying the football on a quick fullback dive play. As soon as the fullback has cleared the line of scrimmage with his fake, he is coached to look for an opponent to block.

The fullback's soft fold (pocket) allows the quarterback the opportunity to pull the ball out of the fullback's pocket at the last minute. The dive man should not clamp his arms around the ball and try to pull the ball away from the quarterback. The option to give or keep the ball is solely up to the quarterback.

The fullback is responsible to keep the ball from being pushed through the pocket. His right arm and elbow should be two to three inches away from his body, to prevent the quarterback from sticking the ball all the way through the fullback's pocket.

Fullback's Leveled Off Approach

While the fullback dive has been often referred to as "a veer-like path," the fullback actually is coached to hit the line of scrimmage with his shoulders parallel to the goal line. The angle of the veer depends upon the offensive tackle's block. If the offensive tackle blocks the defender to his inside, the fullback is coached to level off sooner than if the offensive tackle, to the point of the attack, is assigned to block the defender directly over the blocker. Regardless of the offensive tackle's block, the fullback's approach path to the crease must be consistently the same so that the quarterback is able to use his exact steps, fake, and view on his first option key.

The blocking pattern of the offensive linemen in the Triple Option series is designed to open up a crease so that the fullback has a chance of breaking away for the long gainer. Diagram 4-2 illustrates the offensive crease.

Fullback's Triple Option Assignment

If the fullback does not get the ball, he is instructed to make a good fake. If he is not tackled, he is coached to be a blocker. The fullback's blocking assignment is to block the first off-colored jersey once he enters the crease; actually, we assign the fullback to block the linebacker or deep back. He is coached to check straight ahead and then look to the inside to seal off any of the backside defensive pursuit.

Whenever the fullback notices the inside linebacker over pursuing, directing his attention on the quarterback keep, or the pitch out maneuvers, the fullback is told to tell the quarterback; then, the quarterback may call the fullback's base play. (Fullback is given the ball on the fullback dive play and our linemen are alerted to this play in the huddle and block their respective defenders. See Fullback Dive play in Chapter 6).

If the fullback does not get the ball from the quarterback and is not tackled at the line of scrimmage, he is taught to use a cut off block on the pursuing linebacker. (Diagram 4-3.)

Against the goal line defense, the fullback is assigned to block the safetyman if the first key does not tackle the faking fullback.

Since the first key is a difficult read for the quarterback, there are times when the fullback goes through the line unmolested; therefore, we tell the quarterback he is never wrong on the Triple Option, because the fullback is now a blocker and he uses a seal off or reach block on the pursuing linebacker to insure success for the keeper or the pitch out. (Diagram 4-4.)

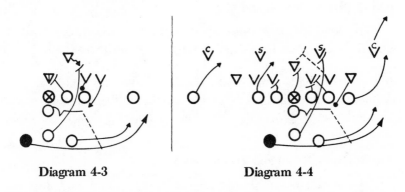

Diagram 4-3   **Diagram 4-4**

The fullback's blocking fundamentals, techniques, and strategy are constantly stressed during practice sessions, as the Triple Option demands that we have eleven blockers on every play. The quarterback is featured as our eleventh blocker, and he does his blocking with his faking.

The fullback's course must be constant, and he cannot change his course until he has reached the crease. Once the fullback passes the quarterback, he is instructed to watch the tackle's block; now, he has the option of altering his course depending upon the block of his offensive tackle.

One coaching point we stress to our fullback is to focus his eyes on the first defensive key (first defender to show outside of the frontside tackle's block). If he keys this defender, he will usually be able to anticipate whether or not he will get the ball from the quarterback. (Diagram 4-5.)

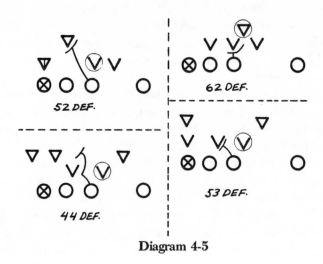

Diagram 4-5

Lead Halfback's Stance and Depth

The lead halfback lines up in a comfortable three point stance with his heels lined up 15 feet from the tip of the football. The three point stance should be balanced so that the weight is evenly distributed over the balls of the feet. The lead halfback's inside foot should be one and one half feet outside of the fullback's near foot. The balanced stance allows the halfback to take off downfield or to the right or left.

Lead Blocker's Route and Techniques

The lead halfback should take a short, parallel lead step with his playside foot and then three steps parallel to the line of scrimmage. All of these steps must be made at maximum speed. After the lead back has taken his three steps, he should begin to turn upfield. Usually the lead blocker looks for the defender who is assigned to contain the sweep or pitchman. He must be ready to force the issue and go after the hesitant defender. Thus, the lead blocker's attacking angle will differ depending upon who is responsible for containing the pitchman and the angle in which the defender attacks the pitch out.

One important coaching point is that the lead back must block any defender who attacks the lead back's path or the lead back himself; thus, we coach the lead back to read the second defensive key (first defender who shows outside the first key). Reading this second key enables the lead halfback to anticipate who will be responsible for containing the pitch out. For example, if the second key attacks the quarterback, the lead halfback focuses his eyes on the next widest defender, for the blocker now knows this next outside defender is responsible to contain the outside play. (Diagram 4-5.)

The lead blocker should strive to get his head, shoulders, and arms in front of the defender and is taught to use a cut down block. The frontside halfback should only use a kick out block on a defender when absolutely necessary. An example would be against the feathering end who is assigned to defend against the pitch out. (Diagram 4-6.)

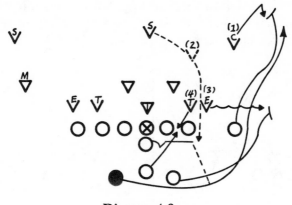

Diagram 4-6

Lead Halfback's Block

The lead blocker drops his inside shoulder slightly, stepping with the inside foot and contacting the defender with the inside hip. The right halfback is coached to keep his head up when pushing off the inside foot, because the defender may try to push the blocker's head down with the inside hand on the blocker's helmet and the outside arm jamming the blocker's outside shoulder. The blocker is also taught to keep his head and his eyes on the defender, because the defensive #2 man may choose to deliver a forearm blast into the intended blocker's numbers. Keeping the head up, the blocker is able to look for this defensive forearm and is able to dip the head under this defensive technique.

The angle of the lead halfback's block depends upon the position of the defender who is responsible to contain the pitch out.

The lead back must be careful not to lunge or commit himself when blocking the containing defender.

Thus, the lead back is coached to place his chop block on the containing defender, only when he is close enough to step on the defender's toes.

Lead Back's Blocking Techniques

The first step should be a short 12 inch parallel step with the lead (right) foot in order to put outside pressure on the defender who is assigned to defend the pitch out. The second step should be taken with the back (left) foot parallel to the line of scrimmage. On the third step with the right foot, the lead halfback should look upfield and train his eyes on the #2 man or the second man from the outside, who is responsible for defending the pitch out. As soon as the lead halfback makes this third step in a staight line, he is coached to make a slight six inch arc and aim for a point one foot outside of the defender responsible for the pitchman. (Diagram 4-7 and 4-8.)

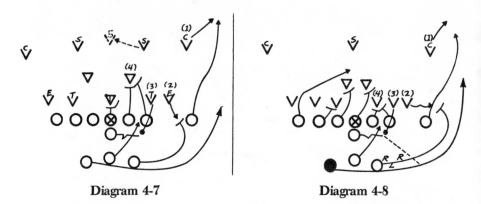

Diagram 4-7   Diagram 4-8

The lead back is coached to make a solid block on the second widest defender, whose responsibility is to contain the pitch out. The width and depth of the right halfback's block is determined by the way the #2 defender reacts to the play. The lead back is taught to attack the outside leg of the defender by extending the inside arm, shoulder, and head outside of the defender's knee. As soon as the inside hip makes contact with the defender's knee, the blocker is coached to aggressively scramble block the defender. Once contact has been made, the blocker should continue his scramble block turning the butt in the progression of the ball carrier. This means that the blockers backside must always be between the blocker and the ball carrier. The blocker is actually taught to aim just above the defender's knee, so that if the defender moves, the blocker will then make contact directly at the defender's knee.

Although the blocker is coached to roll his hips slightly into the defender, we caution the blocker to use an aggressive body block rather than a roll block (where the blocker executes a block by literally rolling at the ankles of the defender).

Some coaches teach the lead halfback to read the second key. The reason for this is that the apparent second key may threaten the lead back's arc. This may be used by blitzing the inside safety on the quarterback and making the defensive end the contain man. Therefore, the actual lead halfback's rule should be "block the second man that *shows* from the outside"; in this case, the defensive end. (Diagram 4-9.)

Blocking The Feathering Defender

When the sweeping ball carrier makes his break to the outside, the deep defender usually tries to shuffle to the outside. As the defender feathers (shuffles) to the outside, he uses his hands to ward off the lead halfback, pushing off the blocker's helmet and shoulder pads. The blocker is coached to break down into a good football position and shuffle to the outside with the defender. Again, the lead back is coached not to attempt to block the deep defender until he makes an attempt to attack the ball carrier. Then, the lead halfback is coached to make his hip block on the defender from his outside-in angle which enables the ball carrier an outside sideline cut. The lead blocker does not place his hip block on the defender until the very last moment. He must be close enough to the defender to step on his toes before he places his block on the shuffling defender. (Diagram 4-10.)

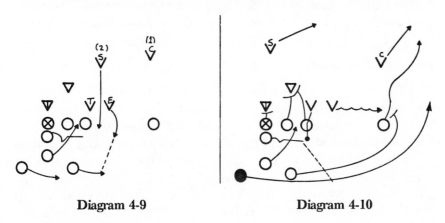

Diagram 4-9   Diagram 4-10

Lead Back's Kick Out Block

Whenever the contain man gains a penetrating depth across the line of scrimmage of four to five yards, the lead halfback is instructed to kick or block this defender outside. There is no way the lead back is able to overthrow this defender and hope that the ball carrier can turn the corner. Since the ball carrier is riding the outside hip of the lead back, he is able to make a quick inside cut and then run to daylight. (Diagram 4-11.)

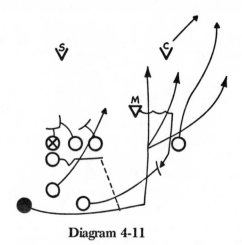

Diagram 4-11

Pitchman's Stance and Depth

The depth of the halfback's heels should be lined up 15 feet from the tip of the football. The halfback's inside foot should be one and one half feet from the near foot of the fullback. The inside hand of the halfback's three point stance is down, with the weight evenly distributed over the balls of the feet. The parallel stance is used so that the halfback is able to take off quickly in any direction.

Pitchman's Assignment

The pitchman uses the same open step technique as we coach the lead back to take. The pitchman is taught to sprint at maximum speed in a straight course through the lead back's original position. The backside halfback should not deviate one step from his straight course or he may throw off the timing of the Triple Option maneuver. After catching the pitch out, we want the ball carrier to shadow the outside hip of the lead back. We want the ball carrier to force the wide sweep to widen the perimeter of the defense. The strategy behind the Triple Option is to get the pitch off wide and make the Big Play go! The ball carrier should cut the play up to the inside only when the defender, responsible for the pitch, has overcommitted himself, forcing the ball carrier to cut the play up inside of the containing defender.

Once the ball carrier breaks outside of the lead halfback's block, the ball carrier is coached to help set up the split end's run off block. Since the coaching staff coaches the split end to maintain outside leverage on the deep one third defender, the ball carrier's inside fake can put the blocker in excellent position to carry out this break away block.

We refer to our lead halfback and split end as our "touchdown makers." This means, if both of these blockers carry out their successful blocking assignments and we get the pitch off, these blockers will make the blocks necessary for a touchdown; therefore, we emphasize the importance of these two men making their blocks by awarding them stars whenever they make their key blocks and we make the touchdown. Daily practice sessions must be spent setting up the different blocking looks the lead back and split end will see versus various defenses. These blockers walk through, jog through, and then run through these blocks in isolated, individual, group, and team drills until their correct blocking rules become a habit.

Once the ball carrier turns the corner, he is taught to favor the outside and then break for daylight. The more knowledge the ball carrier has of the reactions of the various defenders and the blocking assignments of our key blockers, the more intelligent a ball carrier he will become.

The ball carrier is coached to always carry the ball in the outside arm and exchange the ball with two hands from one arm to the other arm. Whenever the ball carrier runs into traffic, he is coached to put both hands over the ball and protect the ball with his shoulders.

Halfback's Triple Option Paths

Both halfbacks are coached to take a lead step with the outside foot and then follow the first step with a crossover step with the inside foot. Coaching emphasis must be placed on the parallel path of both halfbacks. The pitchman must set his course directly through the lead halfback's original position.

Turning The Corner

As soon as the pitchman (trailing back) receives the pitch out, he is coached to turn upfield as quickly as possible. The pitchman is responsible to maintain his four by four yard ration between the quarterback and the trailer; thus, the pitchman must maintain his maximum parallel speed so that no inside defender is able to head off the ball carrier from an inside-out angle.

The pitch out is designed to go around the corner; therefore, the pitchman is coached to stay as wide as possible following his outside lead blocker. As long as the ball carrier remains on the lead back's outside hip, the ball carrier should be able to turn the corner. The only time the ball carrier is instructed to turn upfield inside of the lead block on the containing defender is when the lead back is forced to block out on an outside conscious contain man.

CHAPTER FIVE

Triple Option Line
Blocking Techniques

This chapter deals with the various blocking assignments and techniques for the offensive line. This chapter describes the blocking techniques for a Triple Option play run toward the split end's side. The individual coaching points are described and illustrated for the offensive linemen.

Split End's Triple Option Assignment

The split end's blocking assignment is to block the deep defender who is responsible for the deep outside one third zone. If the secondary is playing a man to man pass defense, the split end is coached to run off the defensive back who is assigned to defend the split end. The split defender lines up eight to ten yards away from the ball and is taught to sprint off the line of scrimmage. His assignment is to run off the deep defender and maintain an outside position on the deep back and keep the defender deeper than his position. Therefore, the split end continues on his outside path as deep as the defender will retreat, while the split man can maintain his outside and shallow leverage position on the deep back. As soon as the defender realizes the pitch has been made and it is a definite wide play, the defender will stop retreating, break down and attempt to attack the sweep. As soon as the defender breaks down, the wide blocker is taught to break down and maintain his two leverage points and not block the deep defender until the defensive man begins to set an upfield course to attack the sweep.

The split end is told to keep his feet until the last moment. The longer the blocker keeps his feet, the more successful the sweep. As long as the split end maintains his two leverage points (wider and shallower than the defender), the blocker may carry out his assignment without ever leaving his feet; thus, the blocker will merely wall off the deep defender.

The split end's assignment is to sprint off the line of scrimmage and look for the defender who will be assigned to defend the deep one third area. If the secondary is playing a zone defense, the deep outside defender normally retreats to his assigned one third zone and the split end is coached to maintain his two leverage points, in front of and wider than the defender. Maintaining these two leverage points enables the split end to cut the defender down from his outside-in position and enables the ball carrier a clear outside path for a touchdown. The split end is coached to sprint downfield and continue sprinting until the deep defender breaks down. Once the blocker breaks down, the split end does not place his block on the defender until the defender commits himself. As long as the deep defender continues to retreat and maintains his big cushion, the split end is taught to continue to sprint downfield. Diagram 5-1 illustrates a four deep zone man to man pass defense.

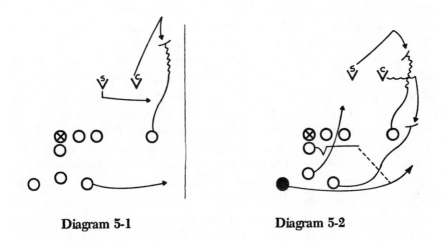

Diagram 5-1   **Diagram 5-2**

If the wide deep defender decides to level off (hangs in the outside one fourth zone), the split end should continue to sprint downfield and look for the next inside defender to rotate into the deep outside one third zone. It is much easier for the split end to maintain the outside position, because he is outside from the very nature of the secondary call. This type of a level call is usually used versus a four deep defense but is also used in a three deep defensive secondary call. Continual practice against this rolling, rotating zone makes it easy for the wide receiver to read these secondary maneuvers. (Diagram 5-2.)

Against the invert or change call, the split end continues downfield and maintains his leverage points on the outside cornerman as illustrated in Diagram 5-1. The only difference is that the inside safetyman rotates up from his position into the outside one fourth zone. When this change call has been made, the lead halfback is responsible to block the inside safetyman, as this defender has now rotated into a role of contain responsibility.

Against the two deep secondary where the five linebackers play the five underneath zones, the split end is still coached to block the defender who is responsible for the deep outside one third zone. Against the two deep safetymen set up, the deep safetymen are assigned deep one half zones so the split end simply carries out his assignment versus the deep safetyman to his side. The split man is cautioned that he may be bumped off his route by the short zone defender who may be assigned to delay the split end. If this is the case, the split end is taught to fake out this defender with a head and shoulder fake. It is best to release outside of this short zone defender so the split man may maintain his outside leverage on the deep secondary defender. (Diagram 5-3.)

If the split end faces the same alignment as previously mentioned and illustrated in Diagram 5-3, he must also realize that the short five defenders may be playing man to man defense from their underneath alignments. The wide receiver is coached to sprint off the line of scrimmage and continue on his outside path, keeping the deep safetyman in front of him and to his inside. The split end is coached to continue sprinting downfield, thus taking both the deep zone defending safetyman and the wide cornerman deep. As soon as the wide cornerman recognizes it is a sweep, the cornerman will then attempt to contain the sweep, and the lead halfback is assigned to block the defending cornerman. (Diagram 5-4.) The outside cornerman may use the bump and run technique against the split end so the wide man must work against this technique in daily practice sessions. In practice, we place the cornerman on the split end's inside shoulder, outside shoulder, and head up so that the split end will have that feeling of "I've been here before." Using these defensive techniques in practice is similar to double coverage methods that may be used by the linebacker. Although few teams use a true double cover technique against the Wishbone offense, we want our split end to be ready on third down and long situations.

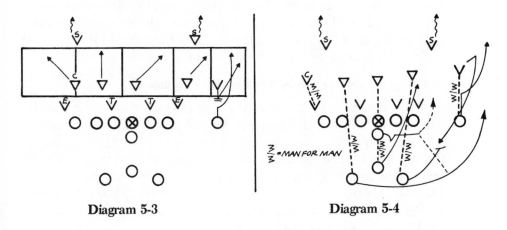

Diagram 5-3   Diagram 5-4

While not many defensive teams rotate from the three deep defense, the split end uses the same path and blocking techniques as illustrated in Diagram 5-2. If the three deep secondary is assigned their normal drop back three deep zones, the split end blocks his deep one third defender maintaining his two yard ratio (outside and in front of the deep defender) leverage as illustrated in Diagram 5-1

Split End's Block

The split end is assigned to block the man who lines up on him or the next deep defender to the inside. Once the pitch has been executed, the split end must maintain his outside position and keep the defender responsible for the deep outside one third zone in front of him. The wide receiver should continue to stay on his feet and chug the defender until he is forced to leave his feet and place a block on the defender.

If the split end's assigned defender is using a leveling technique, it means the defensive safetyman is assigned to revolve and cover the deep outside one third zone. The split end is assigned to pass up the leveling defensive back and block the defender who is sprinting into the deep outside one third area.

The split end must determine who the #1 man is. He is the defender who will cover the deep outside one third zone. The wide man must set his downfield course to keep this defender deeper and inside of the split end. The split end is coached to sprint downfield on his course as deep as the defensive back continues to maintain a cushion on the split end. As soon as the deep back recognizes a sweep play is developing, he normally breaks down to react to the wide play. The blocker is also taught to break down and maintain his outside leverage and stay between the ball carrier and the deep defender.

The split end does not try to block the defender until the deep back attempts to head off the blocker. Only then should the split end place his hip block on the defender and cut him down.

Frontside Tackle's Triple Option Blocking Techniques

The frontside tackle's blocking assignment is: *Inside, linebacker.* This wall off block by the offensive tackle helps to wall off the interior defenders, creating a running crease for the fullback dive maneuver. (Diagram 5-5.) The frontside tackle is coached to release with the inside foot on a 45 degree angle. If a defender lines up directly over the offensive tackle, he is coached to drive through this #4 defender's inside leg, driving upfield to help wall off the inside defensive linebacker versus an Oklahoma defense.

Playside Tackle

The frontside (playside) tackle is coached to take a short lead step with his inside foot and set a course to cut off the frontside linebacker. The blocking tackle is taught to fire for the linebacker where he will be, rather than where he is. The normal Oklahoma linebacker will scallop (shuffle) in the direction of the flow of the offensive backs. Therefore, the frontside tackle's second (right foot) step should be directed on an upfield angle to cut off or wall off the shuffling defender. (Diagram 5-6.) The blocker's route normally is a 45 degree angle; but if the linebacker shuffles toward the play, the frontside tackle may have to follow the linebacker driving his helmet into the defender's back. As the linebacker continues to scallop away from the chasing offensive tackle, the blocker is coached to stick to the defender and drive him beyond the crease. (Diagram 5-7.)

The frontside tackle steps with his inside foot first to give the quarterback a quicker and clearer picture of the ball handler's first key. Some Triple Option coaches teach the tackle to step with the outside foot first, expecting the defensive tackle to veer down and over the frontside offensive tackle. The outside step can help the blocker fight through the defensive tackle's pinching technique; but, we feel that the step with the inside foot helps the quarterback's view of his first key (first defender outside of the offensive tackle).

If the defensive tackle is playing a #4 technique (head up on the offensive tackle) and is holding up the playside tackle's release, the tackle is coached to drive upfield through the defender's inside leg.

This gives the blocker power to meet the defender's chug and gives the offensive tackle a better angle on the scrapping inside linebacker. (Diagram 5-8.)

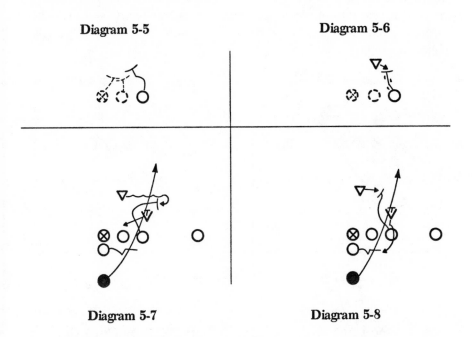

Diagram 5-5

Diagram 5-6

Diagram 5-7

Diagram 5-8

The diving fullback is also coached to seal off the shuffling or scrapping inside Oklahoma linebacker by taking a course outside of the offensive tackle's block. This usually happens when the defensive tackle pinches across the frontside tackle's face. The frontside tackle is coached to block the pinching defensive tackle, who is also blocked by the frontside offensive guard. Now the fullback goes outside of the tackle's block and picks off the scrapping inside linebacker. (Diagram 5-9.)

The first lead step with the inside foot helps the offensive tackle's cut off angle to intercept the straight blitzing inside linebacker. (Diagram 5-10.) The frontside tackle must set his course to intercept the potential blitz by the Oklahoma linebacker, because a prerequisite of a successful Triple Option play is to stop any defensive penetration.

The offensive guard may make a call whereby the center will block the middle guard by himself, and the frontside guard and frontside tackle will both double team the inside linebacker. Both of the offensive blockers will try to drive the linebacker directly backwards to cut off or wall off the flow of the backside Oklahoma linebacker. (Diagram 5-11.) The frontside tackle drives off his inside foot and sets a course to drive his left shoulder into the defender's numbers and puts his head on the outside of the linebacker's outside hip. The blocking tackle is then taught to swing his hips toward the posting guard's snoot block. This move squares both blockers' shoulders parallel to the line of scrimmage and drives the defensive linebacker straight back into the pursuit path of the backside defensive pursuit. (Diagram 5-11.)

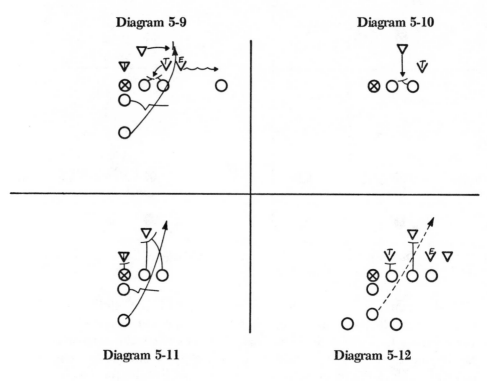

Diagram 5-9   Diagram 5-10

Diagram 5-11   Diagram 5-12

The frontside blocking tackle must fire to his inside and not be delayed on the line of scrimmage. If the defensive tackle is able to hold up the offensive tackle, the quarterback will have difficulty in reading his first defensive key.

The frontside offensive tackle is normally coached to block to his inside; but, he is also taught that he should leave only two defenders outside of him on or near the line of scrimmage. Therefore, the playside tackle realizes he must block a defender directly over himself if there are only two men to his outside. One illustration of blocking the man head up on the playside tackle is the 62 defense. (Diagram 5-12.)

If the frontside offensive tackle would block to his inside and help the offensive guard to double team the defensive tackle directly over the guard, there would be three defenders left on or near the line of scrimmage outside of the offensive tackle's block. This means that the inside 62 linebacker could take the fullback, the end could veer in and tackle the quarterback, and the outside linebacker could attack the pitch out. (Diagram 5-13.)

The Triple Option can still be run against this defense, but it would not give the quarterback a true Triple Option in the actual or literal sense.

Therefore, our offensive staff coaches the frontside tackle to block the linebacker directly over him and teaches the fullback to run a slightly wider path. This widens the crease slightly. (Diagram 5-14.)

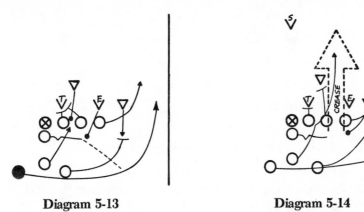

Diagram 5-13   Diagram 5-14

This forces the defensive end to attack the fullback, and the outside linebacker must defend against the quarterback; therefore, the quarterback makes the pitch and the ball carrier has turned the corner with both the tight end and lead halfback blocking against the one deep secondary defender.

Against the gap defense, the playside tackle is coached to block the defender in the inside gap. The frontside tackle must take a sharp blocking angle to cut off the gap defender's gap charge.

Diagram 5-15   Diagram 5-16

In blocking the 44 defense the playside tackle uses one of these blocks:

1. Fold block   (Diagram 5-15)
2. Double team   (Diagram 5-16)
3. Combo block   (Diagram 5-17)
4. Block linebacker   (Diagram 5-18)

Diagram 5-17   Diagram 5-18

Frontside Tackle's Triple Option "Looks"

The following ten offensive tackle's looks are diagrammed and numbered pertaining to the defender's alignments and defensive techniques. (Diagram 5-19.)

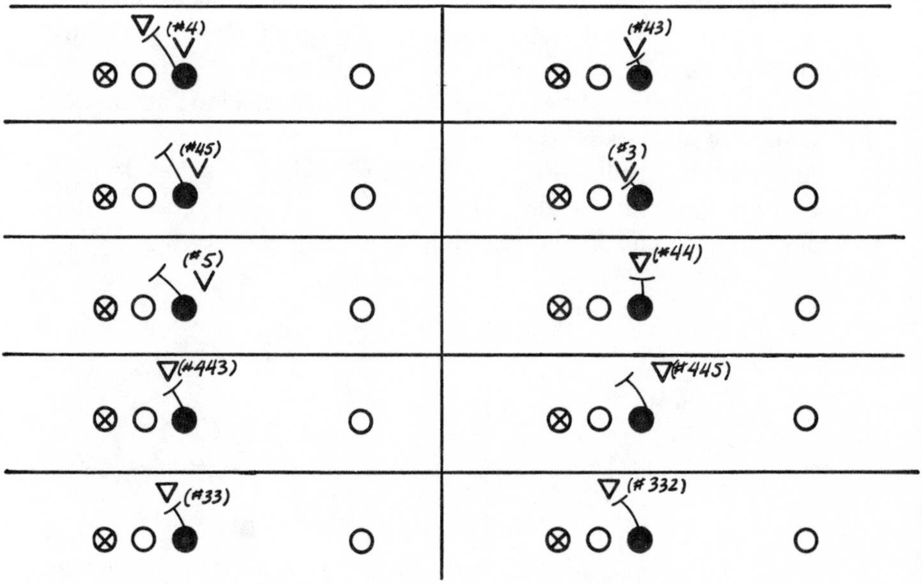

Diagram 5-19

Frontside Tackle's Blocking Test Chart

Diagram 5-20 illustrates a test chart which is issued to our offensive tackle. The blocker is issued the chart, and it is his responsibility to draw his blocking assignments against each defense.

The play drawn up is Triple Option Right, and the offensive tackle has drawn in both the guard and himself to the point of attack. We ask our offensive tackle to draw in their guard's block because his knowledge of the frontside guard's assignments make the frontside tackle a better blocker. See Diagram 5-20: Frontside Tackle's Test Chart—Play: Triple Right.

Frontside Guard's Triple Option Blocking Techniques

The playside (frontside) guard's blocking assignment is to block the #1 defender. At times the playside guard may block the #1 defender by himself, and at other times he will have help from the playside tackle.

Since the playside guard is in a middle position between the center and the playside tackle, the guard is also assigned to make the Triple Option blocking calls for the interior offensive linemen. Thus, if the offensive guard needs help on the #1 defender, he calls on the playside tackle to help double team the #1 defender. If he can take him by himself, he allows the playside tackle to simply follow his normal blocking assignment.

Playside Guard's Drive Blocks

The frontside guard's release block is used when there is no down defender in the inside gap or directly over the guard. The release block technique is featured by stepping with the inside foot toward the offensive center. The inside foot should be aimed at the middle guard's near hip. If the middle guard stunts toward the frontside guard, the blocker is coached to block the defender using his head on blocking technique. (Diagram 5-21.) If there is no middle guard or the middle guard stunts away from the blocker, he is coached to readjust his path and cut off the backside linebacker. (Diagrams 5-22 and 5-23.)

Blocking The Middle Stacked Linebacker

One exception to the previous rules is, whenever the linebacker is stacked behind the middle guard, the frontside guard is taught to block the middle linebacker while the center blocks the middle guard by himself. (Diagram 5-24.) We see a lot of this middle stack when an opponent uses the 44 or Split-40 defense and one of the middle linebackers moves to a down position on the nose of the offensive

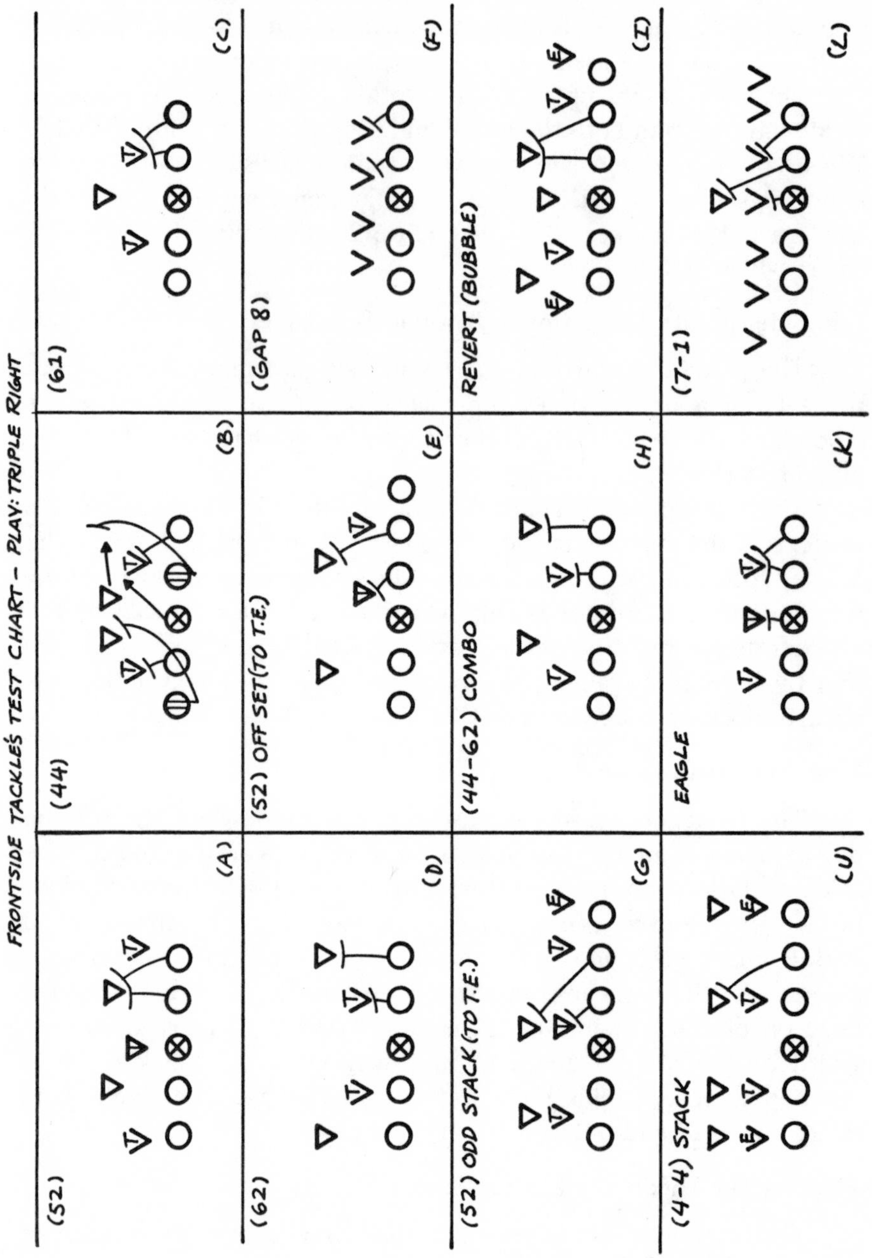

FRONTSIDE TACKLE'S TEST CHART – PLAY: TRIPLE RIGHT

(52) (A)   (44) (B)   (61) (C)

(62) (D)   (52) OFF SET (TO T.E.) (E)   (GAP 8) (F)

(52) ODD STACK (TO T.E.) (G)   (44-62) COMBO (H)   REVERT (BUBBLE) (I)

(4-4) STACK (J)   EAGLE (K)   (7-1) (L)

Diagram 5-20

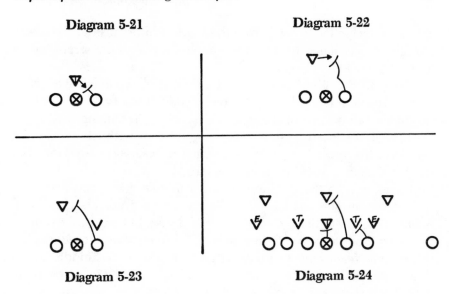

Diagram 5-21   Diagram 5-22

Diagram 5-23   Diagram 5-24

center, and the other inside linebacker moves to a stacked position directly in back of the nose defender. (Diagrams 5-25 and 5-26.) This defense then becomes a 7-Diamond or 53 defense, depending upon whether the two outside linebackers play on the line of scrimmage in a seven man line technique (7-Diamond defense in Diagram 5-25) or both outside linebackers move off the line of scrimmage in a five man defensive line with three linebackers (53 defense in Diagram 5-26).

Diagram 5-25   Diagram 5-26

44 Blocking

The guard is coached to step with the near foot on a 45 degree angle, aiming his helmet just outside of the blocker's thigh. If the defender stays low, the blocker is coached to aim his head just outside of the defensive tackle's knee. Once the offensive guard makes contact, he is coached to scramble on all fours cutting off the defender's lateral movement forcing the defender upfield. The blocker's body should then point directly toward the goal line, and then the blocker is taught to turn his butt in progression of the ball carrier. If the defensive tackle loops away from the blocker to the inside, the offensive guard is coached to continue upfield for one of the scrapping off inside linebackers. (Diagram 5-27.)

Usually the offensive tackle will check block the defensive tackle; and, if the defender does not loop outside, the offensive tackle is taught to wall off one of the inside linebackers. (Diagram 5-27.)

The frontside (playside) guard should step with his inside foot and drive his inside ear past the nose guard's near side hip. Once the blocker's head is past the middle guard, he is coached to swing his butt over next to the double teaming middle guard and drive the nose defender straight backward. We want the frontside guard and offensive center to drive the middle guard straight backward to cut off the pursuit of the backside linebacker. There is a strong tendency for the double teamming guard to attempt to drive the middle guard away from the crease by pushing the defender on a 45 degree angle away from the point of attack. (Diagram 5-28.)

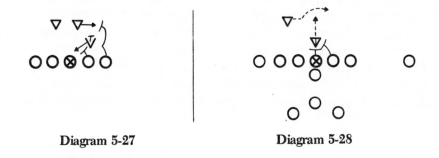

Diagram 5-27   Diagram 5-28

Double Team Block

The drive man (frontside guard) is coached to take a lead step with the inside foot directly at the defender's near side hip. Once the frontside offensive guard feels defensive pressure, the defender is taught to rotate his hips toward the defender to seal off the double team block.

The center is the post man, and he is coached to block the defender just as he would on a one-on-one block. The blocker must neutralize the defender's charge, and the drive man (frontside guard) is expected to drive down on the defender and drive the defender backward while sealing off the crease.

Play Off Block

The frontside guard must fire out under control, because the middle guard may stunt away from the blocker and then the blocker must look up the backside inside linebacker. As soon as the noseman stunts away, the playside guard is coached to take a wider angle and go for the backside inside linebacker where he will *be* rather than where he *is*. Therefore, the blocker must maintain a position which puts him between the scalloping backside Oklahoma linebacker and the ball carrier; thus, the frontside guard walls off the backside linebacker's pursuit. (Diagram 5-29.)

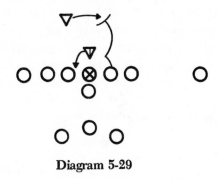

Diagram 5-29

Center's Triple Option Blocking Techniques

The center rule is to block the #0 man or frontside or backside gap. If the defender is nose up in a #0 position like in an Oklahoma middle guard, the center is coached to step first with his frontside (playside) foot. The frontside step is necessary to cut off a stunting middle guard and puts the blocking man between the defender and the ball. If the #0 defender plays normal (delivers a blow on the center then reacts to the play) or plays soft (waits on the line of scrimmage and then flows toward the ball), the center is taught to drive for the defender's playside hip. His first step is with the frontside foot, and then the blocker should shoot his head and backside arm in front of the nose up defender. As soon as the blocker shoots his head and shoulders between the defender and the ball, he should then break down into his scramble blocking position. This position places the blocker on all fours, and he should make contact on the defender with his backside hip and continue to scramble on the defender. The blocker should work his way upfield, driving the #0 defender straight back upfield thus forcing the backside Oklahoma inside linebacker to scallop around the center's scramble block.

If the middle guard attempts to jump over this scramble block, the center is coached to raise up his butt to trip up any hurdling attempt by the #0 defender. The scramble blocker must aim low enough to stay lower than the defender. If the defensive middle guard is able to get his forearm blast under the center's block, the #0 defender has an advantage over the potential blocker. Once the center has made contact on the middle guard, he must continue to scramble aggressively after the head on defender. The blocker is then coached to turn his butt in progression to the ball carrier. This technique keeps the blocker's body always between the defender and the ball carrier.

Contact must be established with the blocker's backside hip, driving into the defender as the blocker steps with the same backside foot. The inside shoulder must be dropped so that the blocker dips below the defender's potential forearm blow. The blocker must keep his head up slightly and never be forced to go to his knees. The blocker must have quick feet and even quicker hands. If the blocker's hands are not moving quickly enough, he may get them stepped on by the defender. (Diagram 5-30.)

Diagram 5-30

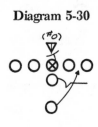

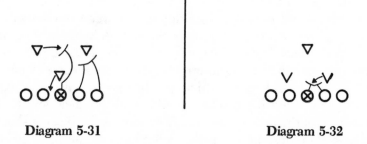

Diagram 5-31   **Diagram 5-32**

The center may get help from the frontside guard's double team block, but the offensive center is coached to be prepared to block the noseman by himself. If the frontside guard does double team block the middle guard, the center continues his leg drive and both blockers are taught to block the noseman directly backward to cut off the pursuit of the backside inside linebacker.

If the middle guard loops or slants away to the backside, the center is coached to continue forward and cut off the backside inside

Oklahoma linebacker. (Diagram 5-31.)

At times, the offensive center may help pick up the defensive tackle who is playing head up (#2 position) on the frontside guard. This happens when the defensive tackle drives down hard into the offensive center's position. This may result in a double team block as in Diagram 5-32.

The center must also be ready to pick up the frontside (playside) defensive inside, blitzing 44 linebacker. (Diagram 5-33.) The center must use a cut off block in this case.

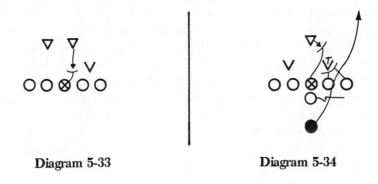

Diagram 5-33   Diagram 5-34

The Cut Off Block

The cut off block is executed by exploding off the near foot, keeping the back parallel to the ground, moving initially forward rather than upward. The blocker's head and backside arm and shoulder should be placed between the defender and the point of the attack. The farside ear should be placed just outside the defenders far hip. The blocker should fire out using short, choppy steps with a wide base to maintain blocking balance. The blocker should drive his head directly upfield and cut off the defender's pursuit toward the point of the attack. The blocker is coached to maintain contact until the whistle blows. The only way this blocking technique can be achieved is to emphasize quick feet at the explosion, contact, and during the follow through techniques.

Center's Chop Block Technique VS. Inside Linebacker

The offensive center is coached to explode off his near foot for the middle linebacker. The center is coached to take a 45 degree angle and shoot for where the middle linebacker will be rather than where he is. This path takes the center through the frontside or playside gap. This playside or frontside course also cuts off the defensive playside tackle if he decides to fire down or loop to the inside. (Diagram 5-34.)

If there is a gap stack to the playside, the center must be ready to help double team this gapped defender. (Diagram 5-35.)

Backside Guard's Triple Option Blocking Techniques

The backside guard is assigned to block the defender in the backside #1 area. The off side guard's #1 assignment usually lines up as a (1) linebacker, (2) gap defender, or a (3) down lineman.

Blocking The Linebacker

1. The backside or offensive guard is coached to step with his inside foot and set a course for the inside hip of the middle guard. Actually, we teach the backside guard to try to get a piece of the middle defensive guard; then, the offensive guard turns upfield and tries to get his head in front of the scalloping, backside linebacker. The offside guard must keep his feet until he is in a good position to cut off the backside defensive linebacker, because the defender is coached to shuffle laterally and backward in arc-like maneuvers to ward off the blocker with his hands. The best method to block this type of a moving linebacker is to use a low scramble-like block and chop down the defender. The quick read of all the backs going away from the defensive backside linebacker starts him quickly in the direction of the point of the attack. Thus, the backside offensive guard must go for a point where the defender will be rather than where he is prior to the snap of the ball. (Diagram 5-36.)

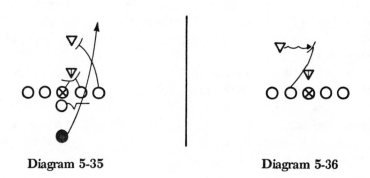

Diagram 5-35   Diagram 5-36

The blocker must be taught to fire out with the inside foot and shoot for the middle guard's inside hip in case the middle guard decides to step around the center's block and shoot through the #1 gap between the middle guard and the backside offensive guard. This path also sets the correct course for the offensive guard to cut off the backside linebacker. (Diagram 5-37.)

Diagram 5-37

The blocker is coached to use a low body block on the shuffling backside linebacker by getting his head and inside shoulder in front of the blocker's far hip. The block is coached to fire for the far hip of the defender but will usually make contact on the far knee of the scalloping backside linebacker. This firing long body blocking technique forces the defensive linebacker to take a wider lateral arc, and then the blocker is coached to roll three times after he has made contact with the scalloping defender. The three rolling technique helps to pin down the blocker who has been cut off his feet, while the three roll offensive blocking technique forces the defensive linebacker to put his hands down upon the blocker, which in turn forces the defender to look at the potential blocker, thus loosing sight of the ball carrier.

The backside guard may also be assigned to block a linebacker in a backside 44 inside linebacker position. Again the backside guard uses his low chop cut off block, and he must take a sharp angle to cut off this linebacker.

2. If the defender is in the frontside guard's inside gap, the blocker reaches on the defender and makes his cut off block. This cut off block has been previously explained under the section "Center's Triple Block Technique."

3. The backside guard uses his head-on block to block the down lineman #1 defender. This defender may be lined up on the outside shoulder of the backside guard. (Diagram 5-38.) If the defender is

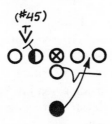

Diagram 5-38

lined up in a #4 technique (head up on the backside guard), the blocker is coached to fire his head at the outside hip of the defender to cut off the defender's pursuit. The blocker then shoots out on all fours, keeping his body between the ball carrier and the defender. (Diagram 5-39.)

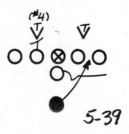

Diagram 5-39

Backside Tackle's Triple Option Blocking Techniques

The backside tackle's assignment is to release inside the backside #2 defender when possible and block shallow in front of the point of attack. Against the Oklahoma defense, the backside offensive tackle is assigned to release inside or outside of the backside inside linebacker and to set a shallow course in front of the point of attack. Since the blocker does not know the exact point of the attack, he is taught to set a shallow course to bring him in front of the middle deep one third area. He then turns upfield slowly and looks for the first odd colored jersey that shows in this one third area. (Diagram 5-40.) If the fullback gets the ball, the blocker simply turns downfield and lead the ball carrier. If the quarterback keeps the ball, the backside blocking tackle may take a flatter course toward the point of the attack and lead the ball carrying quarterback downfield. If the quarterback gets the pitch off, the crossfield blocker is able to see the pitch with peripheral vision and takes his flat course wider to the outside and blocks the defender in the deep one third area. (Diagram 5-41.) The crossfield course the blocker takes from his assigned shallow one third position is dictated by the depth of the deep defenders, when he reacts to the ball carrier.

The backside tackle against the 44 defense may also be assigned a reach call. The reach call assigns the backside tackle to get his head on the inside hip of the backside #2 defender and works his way upfield to cut off the defender's pursuit. Working the blocker's head upfield puts the backside offensive tackle's head in between the defender and the ball carrier, forcing the defender to step deep before he begins to think about his pursuit course.

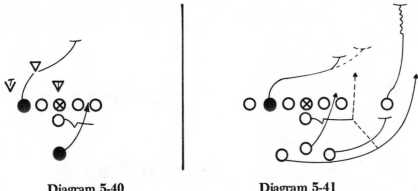

| Diagram 5-40 | Diagram 5-41 |

This block is referred to by our staff as a scoop block. The scoop block often resembles a cut off block, only the scooping blocker continues to work his head upfield. A four point scrambling blocking technique is also encouraged for the scoop blocking technique. (Diagram 5-42.)

Some Triple Option coaching staffs assign the backside tackle to block the backside #2 or #3 defender, rather than going across field to block in front of the point of attack. Their reasoning is that it tires out the backside offensive tackle. We feel that since the offensive tackle is only playing one half of the game (platoon football), he continually should be in fine physical shape to make the crossfield block. We realize it is a difficult block, but if he is successful only once or twice during the game, it may produce one or two scores.

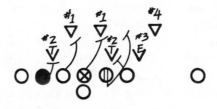

(BACKSIDE T-"REACH CALL")

Diagram 5-42

CHAPTER SIX

How to Run the

Wishbone's Triple Option

The Triple Option is the basic play used in the Wishbone attack. With specific blocking adjustments against different defenses, depending upon their particular player personnel, the Triple Option play can be even a more explosive offensive weapon. The following blocking methods and techniques are discussed and illustrated in addition to the quarterback's optioning techniques.

Running The Wishbone's Triple Option

The double team block on the middle guard is one way of blocking the Oklahoma defense. (see Diagram 6-1.)

The offensive center and frontside guard double team the middle guard. The frontside tackle walls off the Oklahoma linebacker to create the Triple Option "crease." The backside guard blocks the backside linebacker, and both the backside offensive tackle and end sprint across field to their previously described assignments.

If the defensive tackle to the point of the attack takes the fullback, the quarterback is coached to keep the ball and focus his eyes on his second key, the defensive end. If the defensive end attacks the quarterback as in Diagram 6-1, the quarterback pitches to the trailing halfback. The frontside back blocks the defensive cornerman who attempts to contain the wide sweep, and the split end takes his outside-in course to slow block the deep defender who is responsible for the deep outside one third area.

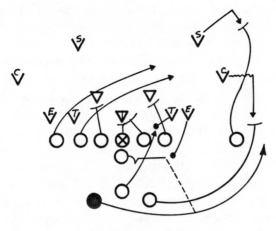

Diagram 6-1

Against a slanting Oklahoma defense, the frontside tackle is coached to block the defender who crosses his face; therefore, if the defensive tackle closes down toward the offensive center, the blocking tackle simply blocks the defender the way he wants to go. If the middle guard also slants or loops away from the point of the attack, the frontside guard is coached to step toward the defensive middle guard and then correct the blocking angle to pick up the backside scalloping linebacker. The offensive center stays with the middle guard if the blocker is unsure of the movement of the middle guard. The backside guard steps with his inside foot toward the offensive center and picks up the slanting or looping middle guard, who is attempting to shoot the backside gap between the backside guard and offensive center. (Diagram 6-2.)

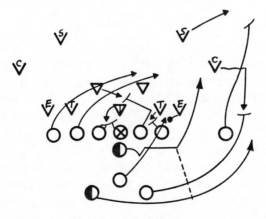

Diagram 6-2

If the defensive end attacks the fullback, the ball handler keeps the football and continues to carry out his Triple Option assignment; but, if the defensive end decides to tackle the quarterback, the ball handler hands the ball off to the fullback. This forces the frontside defensive linebacker to attack the fullback from an inside-out angle; one mistake using this defensive technique, and the fullback will break away for a long gainer. (Diagram 6-2.)

Whenever the quarterback recognizes the first key (defensive tackle) closing inside of the offensive tackle, he checks for the first defender to show outside of the first key. If he recognizes the frontside inside linebacker scrapping into this second key area to attack the fullback on the line of scrimmage, the quarterback may keep the ball and look for the quarterback's second defensive key (defensive end). (Diagram 6-3.) The quarterback occasionally gives the fullback the ball, and he is able to cut inside of the quick scrapping linebacker and break through for a long gainer.

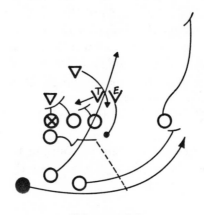

Diagram 6-3

The one-on-one blocking assignment is also used versus the Oklahoma defense, which features each interior offensive blocker to the side of the point of the attack blocking the defender over the blocker. This is usually used whenever the defensive tackle to the frontside lines up just to the inside of the frontside offensive tackle. When this defense presents itself, the frontside tackle blocks the defensive tackle, and the frontside guard blocks the inside linebacker directly over him. The center cuts off the middle guard by getting his head in between the middle guard and the ball. The backside guard is taught to step toward the center to insure cutting off an attempted blitz by the backside inside linebacker; then, the backside guard is coached to take the proper angle to cut off the backside linebacker. The blocker must set his course for where the linebacker will be rather than where the defender is. (Diagram 6-4.)

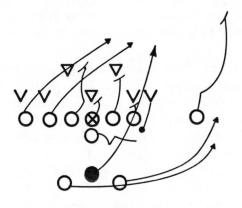

Diagram 6-4

Since the defensive tackle has been blocked in Diagram 6-4, the fullback will receive the ball as long as the defensive end attacks the quarterback. If in the confusion the quarterback failed to hand off the ball to the fullback, the quarterback simply focuses his eyes on the defensive end. If the defensive end decides to contain the sweep, naturally the quarterback would merely keep the ball himself and head upfield. (Diagram 6-5.)

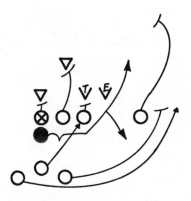

Diagram 6-5

The lead (frontside) halfback and the split end continue to block their regular wide Triple Option assignments just as though the quarterback has made his pitch out. The coaching point behind these assignments is that we always take the pitch whenever our opponents give us the wide play. The quarterback may also wish to pitch the ball to the trailing halfback downfield, past the line of scrimmage.

Blocking the 44 or Split-40 defense can be accomplished in the following manner:

First, the Co-op block is used against the defensive tackle to the side of the point of attack. The frontside guard is coached to fire directly into the defensive tackle's numbers and execute his head-on blocking technique. The blocker is taught to expect to block the 44 defensive tackle by himself. The frontside defensive tackle is coached to use his drive block technique and shoot for the crest of the ilium (hip) of the defensive tackle, and slide off the blocker (if the offensive frontside guard has cut off the defender's penetration and has the opportunity to take the defender by himself). Once the potential drive man on the double team technique is assurred of this fact, the drive man is coached to slide off his drive block and pick up the scrapping frontside, inside linebacker. (Diagram 6-6.) The offensive

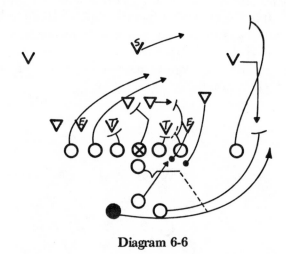

Diagram 6-6

center takes a set step to the playside, looking up a potential blitz by the frontside, inside linebacker through the center-guard gap toward the point of the attack. If there is no blitz, the center sets a course so he can intercept the backside linebacker and wall off his pursuit. The center must be coached to go for the backside, inside linebacker where he will be rather than where he is. The backside offensive guard uses his head-on block on the backside defensive tackle. Both the backside offensive tackle and end take their shallow crossfield courses.

If the defensive end closes down and heads for the fullback, the quarterback keeps the ball. The ball handler then looks for his second key: the outside linebacker. As soon as the outside linebacker commits himself heading for the quarterback, the field general pitches the ball to the trailing halfback. The ball carrying halfback is coached to "ride" the trail of the lead halfback, and the ball carrier's course is determined by the block of the lead back. In this instance (Diagram 6-6.), the lead back picks up the containing outside defensive back, and the third phase of the Triple Option is under way.

Second, the Fold block is used primarily against the 44 defense to utilize the blocking angles of the frontside offensive guard and tackle. If the Fold block is called, the frontside tackle is coached to drive down on the defensive tackle and block him down away from the play. The frontside guard is coached to place his hand on the hip of the drive blocking tackle, and is taught to step around the offensive tackle and look up the scrapping inside defensive linebacker. Once action begins, the frontside inside defensive linebacker is coached to scrape off the tail of the defensive tackle and attack the area, shoulders parallel to the line of scrimmage. The frontside guard should be alert to this defensive technique and be ready to block the linebackers quickly at the crossroads. The offensive guard is coached to slide his head to the outside of the scrapping linebacker, thus sealing off the Triple Option crease. The offensive center is coached to take a step with his outside (playside) foot and then take the proper angle to cut off the backside inside 44 defensive linebacker. A head on block is executed by the backside offensive guard on the defensive tackle on his outside shoulder. (Diagram 6-7.) The backside offensive tackle is unable to release inside of the defensive tackle, because the defensive 44 tackle is coached to play tight on the guard's shoulder and pinch inside through the offensive guard's head. The backside tackle is taught to sprint shallow across field, to the point of the attack, and block the first odd colored jersey. The backside defensive end is coached to go across field and block the defender responsible for the deep one third area. (Diagram 6-7.)

Against the 44 defense, the fronstide scrapping linebacker is often responsible to tackle the fullback from an inside-out position. We feel this is a most difficult assignment for the frontside inside linebacker, or for any other defender to try and stop the fullback from an inside-out angle against the Triple Option play. This is why we use the Fold block. If the defensive end is assigned to tackle the quarter-back, the outside defensive linebacker is then left to contain the pitch out. Usually the outside defender assigned to contain the pitch out uses a feathering technique. This is a quick outside shuffling tech-nique where the defender keeps his shoulders parallel to the line of scrimmage and tries to maintain outside leverage on the lead back. The feathering defender accomplishes this assignment by keeping the lead blocker on his inside shoulder as he shuffles toward the sidelines. The defender's one assignment is to contain the sweep.

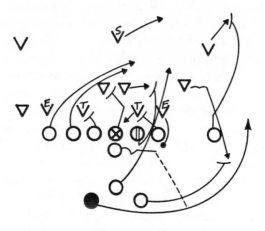

Diagram 6-7

Therefore, the lead halfback must sprint to attempt to get his head on the outside leg of the feathering defender. If the defender beats the blocker to the outside, and there is no possible way the blocker can get to the outside, the halfback is coached to block the shuffling outside linebacker outside in the direction he wants to go. The ball carrier then cuts inside, off the lead back's kick out block.

The split end continues to carry out his assignment by releasing off the line of scrimmage and keeping the defender responsible for the deep outside one third zone in front and to the inside of the blocker. The split end's assignment is consistent whether the lead back kicks out the contain man or over throws on the containing defender.

The fullback (Diagram 6-7) is given the ball, and the Fold block principles allow the ball carrier to break away for a long gainer.

Whenever the offense anticipates an inside linebacker blitz by the 44 defense, the offense features a double team block by the front-side guard and tackle against the defensive tackle. The importance of the double team block against an anticipated inside blitz by the split linebackers is that the defenisve tackles offset the blitz by looping to their outside areas. This means that the defensive tackle to the side of the play will loop out toward the frontside offensive tackle. The double team block will stop his penetration. The outside loop by the backside defensive tackle is blocked by the backside tackle's cut off or seal blocking technique. The center is taught to step with his frontside foot toward the point of the attack, and this places the offensive center in perfect position to pick up the blitzing, frontside inside linebacker. The backside blitzing linebacker who attempts to shoot through the backside offensive guard-center gap can be easily picked up by the backside guard, because his blocking assignment is to take a quick step toward the offensive center and look quickly for the backside inside linebacker to blitz. (Diagram 6-8.)

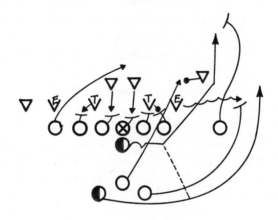

Diagram 6-8

Usually the inside blitz by the shooting linebackers is given away by the linebackers lining up closer to the line of scrimmage. Effective use of the long starting count by the quarterback will often tip off the potential linebackers' blitz by these two defenders' forward movement when the expected starting count is given. A blocking call at the line of scrimmage also alerts the blocking linemen to use a double team block on the defensive tackle toward the point of attack.

Actually the backside offensive tackle has the option of using a cut off block on the looping defensive tackle or passing up the defender and continuing on his way crossfield toward the point of the attack. The option blocking by the backside offensive tackle depends upon the defensive backside tackle's chances of stunting himself completely out of the play. Naturally if the defender loops out of the action, the blocker continues downfield toward his normal assignment.

As soon as the frontside posting offensive guard feels the defensive tackle looping away from the post block, the blocker is coached to attempt to pick up the scrapping frontside inside linebacker. This assignment can be carried out in one of two ways: First, the frontside guard may try to slide through to the inside of the offensive tackle's drive block and attempt to cut off the scrapping linebacker; or, second, the frontside potential post man may fold around the frontside tackle's drive block and cut off the inside linebacker, thus creating a crease for the fullback.

Since the outside linebacker to the side of the point of the attack has been assigned to tackle the fullback and the defensive end has the contain feathering assignment, the inside linebacker must be expected to tackle the quarterback. Therefore, if the frontside offensive guard is able to block the frontside inside linebacker, the quarterback keeper play may become a big play against this 44 defensive stunting action. (Diagram 6-8.)

This is why we preach to our quarterbacks that they must make sure they key the first defender who *shows* outside of the offensive tackle's block. If the quarterback simply keys the first defender outside of the offensive tackle's block, the quarterback would incorrectly give the ball to the fullback as the defensive end begins to scallop to the outside area. Thus, the quarterbacks would continually misread the outside stunts between the outside linebacker and the defensive end.

The quarterback keeper (Diagram 6-8) is most successful if the fullback cuts (blocks) down the inside linebacker. The fullback becomes a blocker as soon as the quarterback does not give the ball to the fullback. The keeper proves most successful as the quarterback continues to sprint away from the defensive pursuit on a 45 degree angle. (Diagram 6-8.)

While we would rather run the Triple Option to the tight end side (Diagram 6-9) because there are fewer defenders, we can still run the Triple Option to the unbalanced side of the defense. The unbalanced defense is blocked in the following manner: The backside offensive end and tackle take their normal crossfield paths. The backside guard and center use their head-on blocks on the defenders over them, while the offensive guard and tackle double team block the frontside, inside Oklahoma linebacker. Since the defensive tackle has been assigned to take the fullback and the outside linebacker has been coached to tackle the quarterback, the lead halfback blocks the mon-

ster defender. The quarterback makes the pitch, and all of the blockers have picked up their assignments (Diagram 6-9) and the backside
halfback has turned the corner.

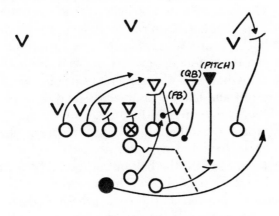

Diagram 6-9

Certainly if the offensive quarterback has the time, he would
automatic the Triple Option away from the overloaded defense to the
split end side (Diagram 6-9) and run the Triple Option to the tight
end side. Running the Triple Option play to the tight end side is
advantageous to the offense as the defense runs out of defenders to
stop the Triple Option maneuver. (Diagram 6-10.)

The tight end swings outside and blocks the defender responsible for the deep outside one third area. His blocking assignment is

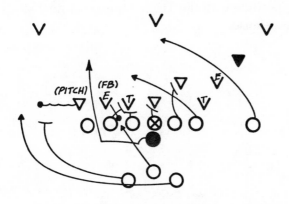

Diagram 6-10

similar to the split end's blocking assignment, keeping the defender in front and to his inside. As soon as the deep defender recognizes it is a run, the blocker breaks down as soon as the defender does and then chops down the deep defender, once this secondary defender commits himself. The offensive tackle drives inside on the defensive tackle and ends up double teamming the defender with the frontside offensive guard. The center and backside guard use their respective head-on blocks on the defenders over them, and the backside tackle sets his course acrossfield shooting for a point just beyond the point of the attack. The split end takes a route acrossfield to block the defender responsible for the deep one third defensive area.

The quarterback fakes the fullback into the crease and reads his first key. As soon as the defensive end fires down on the fullback, the quarterback is taught to pull the ball out of the fullback's pocket and check the ball handler's second key. The second key is the defensive outside linebacker. As soon as the quarterback finds the frontside outside linebacker feathering to the outside, the ball handler is coached to keep the ball and head up the field.

Breaking The Wishbone Backfield

When the Wishbone breaks its backfield to give this attack two wide potential receivers, usually to play catch up football, it can still run the Triple Option. This means the offensive attack can run the Triple Option to the left side as illustrated in Diagram 6-11. But the one half Wishbone is unable to run the Triple Option back to the split end side because there is no back in the trail position. If the offense tries to run the Triple Option right and pitch the ball to the right halfback, the timing would be completely off.

Thus, the one half Wishbone is basically a passing attack and can threaten the opposition with the Triple Option running attack to only one side of the defense.

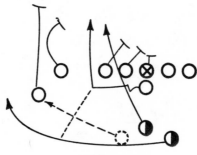

Diagram 6-11

Twin Split Wishbone Formation

The twin split formation is an exciting double width formation which features a strong balanced passing attack, along with the strong Triple Option running attack to either side of the formation. While many defensive coaches view this formation to be primarily a passing formation, it is an excellent formation to run the Triple Option. Since most offensive coordinators would rather run the Triple Option to the split end's side, the double split gives an added running dimension to this offensive set. The two wide split ends have a tendency for the defense to spread their defenders wider, thus opening up the chances for success on the dive, counter, and trap plays. (Diagram 6-12.)

Naturally the passing attack has been strengthened with two wide quick receivers. These two wide defenders help to widen the defensive secondary backfield area responsibility.

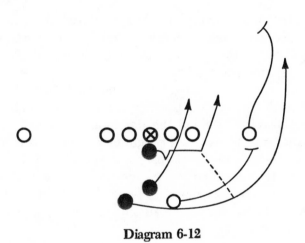

Diagram 6-12

Triple Option Away From 52 Monster Defense

Whenever the opposition employs a monster defender who is assigned to defend the wide side of the field or stationed toward our split end, we like to run the Triple Option to our tight end side. The defense runs out of defenders to cover the Triple Option in an assigned man on man defense. This means the #4 defender (inside linebacker) to the tight end side is responsible to tackle the fullback. When the monster defender is stationed to the split end side, we like to assign two blockers to double team this inside Oklahoma linebacker. This means the #3 defender (defensive tackle) must be assigned to tackle the quarterback. (Diagram 6-13.)

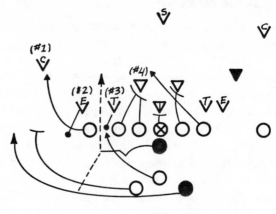

Diagram 6-13

This leaves an automatic hole for the fullback dive, in between the double teammed inside linebacker and the defensive tackle, who is assigned to tackle the quarterback. Actually, the defense to the tight end side runs short of defenders, because the #2 defender (defensive end) must be assigned to stop the third phase of the Triple Option, the pitch out. The deep secondary man to the tight end side must be responsible to defend the deep one third area. Since the defensive ratio breaks down to the tight end's side, this is where we want our quarterback to direct the point of attack. Therefore, if a Triple Option play was called to the wide side of the field (toward the split end) and the monster moved toward this side of the field, our quarterback would be coached to automatic the Triple Option away from the monster.

The Predetermined Triple Pitch Play

Whenever the opposition begins to shut off the fullback dive from the Triple Option, our quarterback is coached to call base triple pitch blocking, which enables the quarterback to pitch or keep the football. This means our quarterback predetermines that we are definitely going for the big quarterback keep or pitch play to the trailing halfback by blocking the first key, who is responsible for the fullback dive. Since the fullback knows he will not carry the ball, he now becomes a more effective blocker and is able to adjust his course, after accepting the quarterback fake, to pick up the most challenging defender. This means against the Oklahoma or 52 defense, the fullback first looks for the defensive tackle, inside linebacker, and then the defensive safetyman. (Diagram 6-14.)

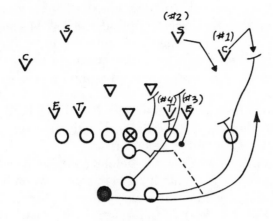

Diagram 6-14

This play is called when the offensive attack wants to force the option play on a particular defense. This play is placed into the offense only after the true Triple Option play has been perfected. This call is particularly good versus the 44 or Split-40 defense, as the fullback's block insures the elimination of the inside linebackers' pursuit and helps to isolate the #3 defender, who is responsible to tackle the quarterback or contain against the pitch out. (Diagram 6-15.)

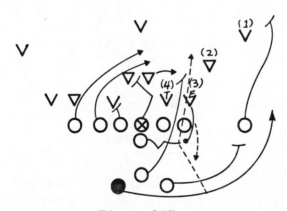

Diagram 6-15

The base call against the second key (#3 man) is also effective, particularly when the opposition has a strong defensive tackle to the point of the attack. This play calls for a double team block by both the frontside offensive guard and tackle on this defensive tackle. The center checks the frontside (playside) linebacker for a possible blitz, then blocks back on the backside (offside) inside 44 linebacker. The fullback, who knows before hand he is not going to get the ball, makes a good fake and then turns up to the inside to block the frontside inside linebacker (Diagram 6-15.) This seal off block by the fullback helps to isolate the #3 defender, so the quarterback can fix a maximum time read on the defender. The base blocking call helps the quarterback to eliminate the inside read on the first key, so he is able to place full attention on the second read.

The base blocking call is also helpful to the quarterback against any stunting defense (particularly the 44 defense) when they stack the outside linebacker behind the defensive end. Now either the #3 defender or the #2 defender may attack the quarterback or the pitchman. This is why we say, "Key the first defender to show outside of the first key." The coaching point behind this statement is that either the #2 or #3 defender may attack the quarterback or attempt to contain against the pitch. (Diagram 6-16.)

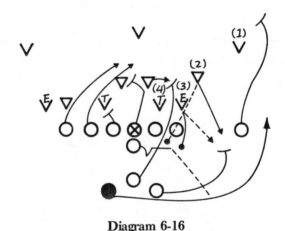

Diagram 6-16

A maximum split by the frontside offensive tackle often breaks down this stack and helps to eliminate the threat of the #2—#3 defensive stunt. If the maximum split does not break down this stack situation, it moves the stack farther away from the quarterback. Thus, the quarterback has a longer look at this stack and is able to make a more intelligent choice as to whether to keep the football or pitch it to the trailing back.

Against the 62 defense, the fullback sets the exact same course for the crease and then takes an adjustment step so he is able to help seal off the inside flow of the defense. (Diagram 6-17.) If the #3 defender attacks the quarterback, he pitches the ball to the trailing halfback who maintains his four-four yard ration from the quarterback. The lead halfback is assigned to go for the outside hip of the #2 defender. The lead halfback takes his first step parallel to the line of scrimmage and stays parallel for the first three steps. On the third step, the lead back must be ready to adjust his angle to get his outside hip on the outside hip of the #2 contain man. The halfback executes a high, hard hip block on the containing defender thrusting his head, shoulders, and arms directly upfield. The blocker is coached to continue to scramble-block the defender. As the blocker scrambles, he is taught to turn his butt in progression of the ball carrier so the defender's pursuit angle is lessened as the ball carrier advances downfield.

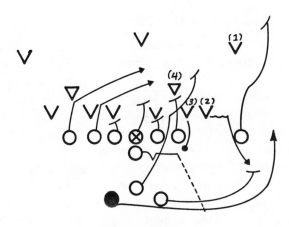

Diagram 6-17

Predetermined Triple Option Pitch

The Predetermined Triple Option Pitch may be consistently successful when running against the Off Set Oklahoma Stack defense, particularly away from the middle guard stack.

Both the frontside guard and tackle are assigned to double team the #1 defender. Since the fullback knows it is a pitch play, he is able to hit his crease and block the inside linebacker, if he is not tackled by the #3 defender. (Defensive End).

The quarterback makes the pitch regardless of the way the first or second keys react, since this is a predetermined play. (Diagram 6-18.)

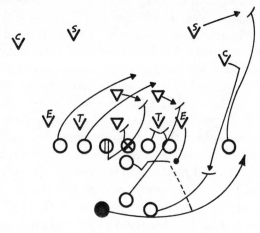

Diagram 6-18

The Predetermined Fullback Dive Play

The dive is the most consistent facet of the normal Triple Option series. The offensive reasoning behind this belief, is, once the dive man is given the ball, he has his assigned option cut off the Triple Option's discriminating line blocking techniques. The dive eliminates the defensive pursuit because the play hits so quickly. The quick give to the dive man freezes the defensive linebackers, which allows the keeper and the pitch more scoring punch. The quick opening dive thrust forces the defensive safetyman to break down right now and become the last defensive tackler between the ball carrier and a touchdown. No longer can the deep secondary defenders be primarily pass defenders and tacklers second. The quick dive forces these deep defenders to hold their retreating techniques to honor the quick dive play.

Predetermined Dive To The Tight End's Side

The definite give to the fullback is called in the huddle and assigns an offensive blocker to block the defender, who is responsible to tackle the fullback. This is our basic call whenever the Triple Option is not running smoothly. Once the precalled fullback dive breaks loose, the Triple Option also begins to break away for the long gainers.

Basically, running the fullback dive to the tight end's side features discriminate blocking and option running. Discriminate blocking means the offensive linemen are coached to block the defender whichever way the defender tries to go. The offensive running back then uses option running and breaks off the offensive lineman's block. (Diagram 6-18.)

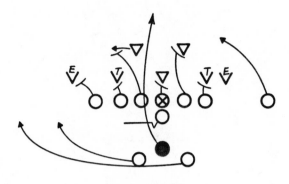

Diagram 6-19

In Diagram 6-19 the left offensive guard blocks the inside Oklahoma linebacker in the direction he is heading, and the fullback breaks inside of the frontside guard's block. The left tackle blocks out on the defensive tackle, and the offensive left end uses his head-on block, turning the defensive end to the outside. The offensive center cuts off the middle guard, getting his head between the nose defender and the point of attack. The defensive linebacker is cut off by the backside guard, and the backside offensive tackle blocks the defensive tackle using his one-on-one blocking technique. The reason the backside defensive tackle is blocked is to insure his being cut off in the event the fullback should decide to cut the dive play all the way behind the middle guard. The offensive cut back by the fullback is often used when the defensive middle guard overpursues to the apparent side of the potential Triple Option attack.

Against the 61 or Pro 40 alignment, the fullback may make his break between the block of the frontside guard and the head-on block by the frontside (left) offensive tackle. Diagram 6-20 illustrates the frontside guard cutting off the head up defender, while the center also cuts off the middle linebacker.

If the defensive tackle to the point of the attack was too strong for the frontside guard to block one-on-one, the offensive guard is coached to ask for help. Thus, the frontside guard would call for a cross block which features a drive block by the frontside tackle on the inside defensive tackle. The frontside guard then delays long enough to clear the drive blocking tackle's hip, and then pulls and kicks out on the defensive end. This cross blocking technique gives both of the

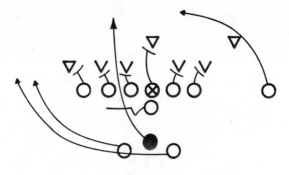

Diagram 6-20

offensive blockers excellent angles for their blocks and opens up a wide hole for the fullback to drive through the crease between his frontside offensive guard and tackle. The frontside offensive end is assigned to turn out on the end man on the line of scrimmage (outside linebacker) and is directed to block the defender away from the point of the attack. (Diagram 6-21.)

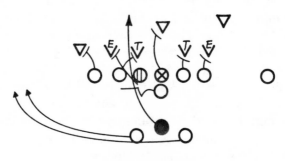

Diagram 6-21

Fullback Dive Blocking To The Split End

The option running of the fullback on the predetermined fullback dive to the split end's side is minimized by the fact that there is no tight end to block. The fullback's outside cut may take the ball carrier so wide he may run into the defender just outside of the frontside tackle's block; thus, the fullback must be coached to run inside of the tackle's block (Diagram 6-22). All of the blocking calls previously explained and illustrated to the tight end's side may also be used to the split end side.

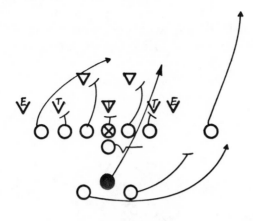

Diagram 6-22

The success of the fullback basic dive plays insures success of the Triple Option pitch play because the defenders must honor the inside dive threat.

Wishbone's Outside Veer

The Wishbone's outside veer runs the option off the outside defender on the line of scrimmage. Against the Oklahoma defense, the frontside offensive tackle and tight end block the defensive tackle. The frontside halfback is the dive man just like the Split Veer Triple Option attack. The fullback runs a course parallel to the line of scrimmage and is assigned to block the defender, who is responsible for containing the pitch out. After the quarterback fakes the ball to the diving frontside halfback, he is then coached to challenge the defender, who is assigned to contain the pitch. If the first defender outside of the double team (end) attacks the dive back, the cornerman (#2) is then responsible to either stop the pitchman or the quarterback. Whatever decision the cornerman makes, he is wrong. If he contains, the quarterback keeps the ball on the keeper for breakaway yardage. If the cornerback (#2) tackles the quarterback, the ball handler pitches the ball back to the trailing halfback, and he has both a fullback and a split end blocking in front of him on only the outside safetyman. (Diagram 6-23.)

Therefore, the fullback and the frontside halfback exchange offensive assignments pertaining to the Triple Option series. The frontside halfback becomes the dive man and the fullback now becomes the lead blocker. The Outside Veer play helps to eliminate the inside defensive pursuit by directing the dive man outside of the end's block, instead of the dive man cutting, more inside, off the offensive tackle's block in the normal Triple Option series.

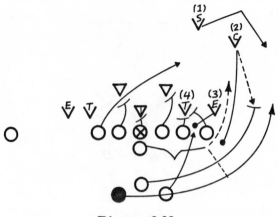

Diagram 6-23

Running the Outside Veer off the Wishbone set against the 44 defense, the key is the outside defensive linebacker's alignment. If the outside linebacker plays the inside shoulder of the tight end, the tight end blocks the linebacker to the inside (Diagram 6-24). If the outside linebacker plays head up on the offensive tight end, the end blocks the defender straight backward.

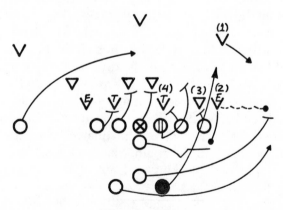

Diagram 6-24

The frontside halfback (dive man) is coached to run a course just to the outside of the far hip of the tight end. The frontside offensive guard folds around the frontside tackle's drive block. The folding offensive guard is then coached to try and seal off the frontside, scrapping inside defensive linebacker. The offensive center reaches on the frontside inside linebacker also. Both the backside offensive guard and tackle reach on the defenders to their inside and attempt to get their heads in front of their respective assignments. (Diagram 6-25.)

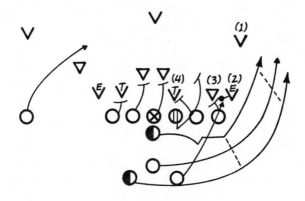

Diagram 6-25

The quarterback checks the reactions of the #2 defender. Since the #2 man is assigned to contain the play, the quarterback gives the ball to the diving halfback, whether the containing defender steps straight across the line of scrimmage or feathers quickly to stop the outside offensive threat. If the quarterback gains too slow a read on the #2 defender so that he is unable to make the hand off to the dive back, he simply keeps the ball inside the containing defender. (Diagram 6-25.)

If the defensive end (#2) makes the mistake and closes in to tackle the fullback, the quarterback can make the pitch, and this will give the ball carrier a lead fullback to block the cornerman (#1); or, the quarterback may decide to keep the ball and turn upfield. As soon as the ball handler turns upfield, the lead fullback and pitchman continue to turn upfield still expecting the quarterback to make the pitch. Now the quarterback challenges the deep (#1) cornerman. The cornerman must make the decision to attack the quarterback or stay outside to contain the pitch out. In either decision, the corner defender is wrong. If the defender attacks the quarterback, the ball handler makes the downfield lateral. If the defender hangs to the outside looking for the lateral, the quarterback merely tucks the ball away and continues downfield toward the goal line (Diagram 6-25.)

The most difficult assignment is teaching the pure Wishbone Quarterback to make the wide veer fake. If the quarterback runs both the Wishbone and Split Veer Series, this technique has been previously taught and no major problem should exist.

CHAPTER SEVEN

How to Block the Deep Secondaries

The quarterback's wide men and lead blockers must be well schooled in all phases of the defenses used to stop the Triple Option. This does not mean just the defensive interior and perimeter, but it also means they must know how the deep back will be assigned to stop the Triple Option. In the following defensive secondary assignments, these offensive players are taught how the deep defenders may be assigned to attack the quarterback or the pitchman. The following is a comprehensive study of how the deep secondaries react to, and attack, the Triple Option.

Defensive Secondary Strategy

The defensive secondary stunts versus the Triple Option must be fully understood by the quarterback, press box coach, and head coach. Game time communications among these three men are essentail to consistently run a successful Triple Option attack. Therefore, our offensive coaches break down the defensive secondaries in two groups: (1) Three deep secondary, and (2) four deep secondary.

Three Deep Secondary Strategy

Against the three deep secondary, we look for four methods whereby these deep backs are able to attack the Triple Option play to the tight end's side.

First: Many three deep secondaries will run a three deep roll or rotating defense where the outside cornerman or halfback will rotate up or roll to the outside as the contain man and the middle safetyman will rotate to cover the deep outside one third area. When this secondary call takes place, the backside cornerman or halfback is responsible for the backside two thirds area. Using this secondary action with the contain responsibility in the hands of the cornerback, the two outside defenders on the eight man line are now free to tackle the fullback and quarterback from their outside-in angles. Diagram 7-1 illustrates the 44 defense using a roll or rotating three deep defense. The outside linebacker is the first key and is assigned to tackle the fullback, while the defensive end is the second key and assigned to stop the quarterback. The cornerman to the tight end's side rolls up to contain the pitch, and the middle safetyman rotates to defend the deep outside one third area and the backside cornerman defends the deep two thirds zone.

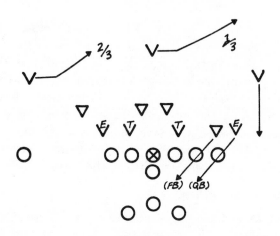

Diagram 7-1

Second: The middle safetyman will play a shallow position, and on flow he will fire up toward the line of scrimmage and be responsible to stop the quarterback. (Diagram 7-2.) The outside linebacker will still defend against the fullback dive and the defensive end feathers to the outside to contain the pitch out. The cornerman to the playside takes the deep outside one third area, while the backside cornerman defends the deep two thirds zone as in Diagram 7-1. Thus, the middle safetyman is the quarterback's second key. This is why we teach our quarterback that the second key is the first defender to *show* outside of the first key.

The middle safety's blitz-like technique is only used by a few deep teams, but we always prepare our quarterback for the unexpected.

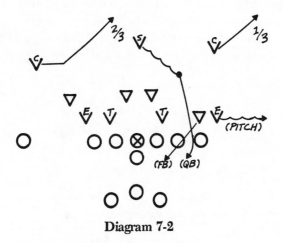

Diagram 7-2

Third: The third secondary maneuver we see from the three deep secondary alignment is an invert-like look from the middle safetyman. Usually the middle safetyman lines up shaded to the tight end's side, particularly if the tight end is to the wide side of the field. (Diagram 7-3.) All of the other defensive assignments are similar to Diagram 7-2.

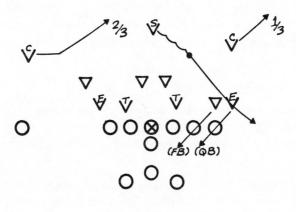

Diagram 7-3

Fourth: From the three deep secondary alignment, the cornerback may also be assigned to tackle the quarterback. This technique calls for the cornerman to veer in from his corner position, attempting to confuse the quarterback who may be looking for the defensive end to attack the ball handler. Since the defensive end is assigned to contain the potential pitch out, the quarterback must focus his eyes on the second key area rather than a particular defender. The middle safetyman contains the deep outside one third area and the backside cornerman is assigned the deep two thirds zone. (Diagram 7-4.)

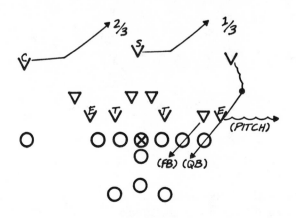

Diagram 7-4

Some 44 defenses attempt to stop the fullback by using one of the inside linebackers, but we feel any defensive team that assigns a defender to stop the fullback consistently from an inside-out angle is asking for trouble. Our coaches believe that the only successful way to stop the fullback on the Triple Option series is from the outside-in angle.

Four Deep Secondary Strategy

The four deep secondary features a seven man defensive front. The four deep secondary may be a man to man or zone pass defense. Against the four deep zone pass defense, we have faced our possible secondary maneuvers.

First: The rolling or revolving pass defense features the cornerman as the containman. The playside safety is assigned to defend the deep outside one third area with the backside safety taking the deep one third middle zone. The backside cornerman covers the backside deep one third zone. (Diagram 7-5.) Thus, the four deep revolving zone always ends up in a three deep zone once the ball has been put into play, since one of the deep four defenders is assigned to contain the pitch out or tackle the quarterback if the ball handler keeps the ball beyond the first defensive key.

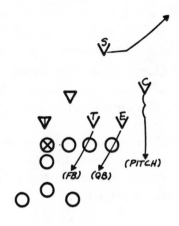

Diagram 7-5

If the defensive front is using an Oklahoma defense, the defensive tackle would be the first key and would be assigned to tackle the fullback from an outside-in angle. The defensive end toward the playside is assigned to tackle the quarterback. (Diagram 7-5.)

Second: Diagram 7-6 illustrates the invert-look where the playside safetyman is assigned to contain the wide play from his inside-out position. The cornerman to his side takes the deep outside

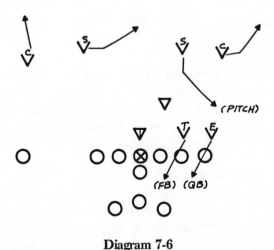

Diagram 7-6

one third zone to his side, while the backside safety is assigned to defend the deep middle one third area. The backside cornerman takes the deep outside one third defensive area to his side.

Again the defensive tackle is assigned to stop the fullback, and the defensive end is taught to tackle the quarterback if he keeps the ball beyond the first key. (Diagram 7-6.)

Third: The third illustration features the frontside safetyman assigned to tackle the quarterback. (Diagram 7-7.) All of the other three defensive backs rotate to their respective three deep areas the same as in Diagram 7-5.

The defensive tackle is still assigned to tackle the diving fullback, but now, the defensive end is taught to tackle the quarterback. The defensive end is coached to feather to the outside to contain the expected pitch out. (Diagram 7-7.)

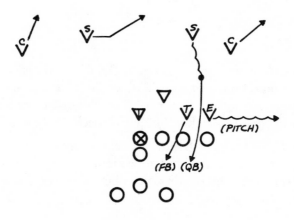

Diagram 7-7

Fourth: The final four deep diagram pictures the frontside defensive cornerman and safety trading assignments in comparision to Diagram 7-7. Now the defensive cornerman is assigned to attack the offensive quarterback, while the playside defensive safetyman is coached to cover the deep outside one third zone to his side. (Diagram 7-8.) The other two backside defensive backs are coached to carry out the same assignments as in Diagram 7-7.

The defensive linemen use the same techniques and assignments as used in Diagram 7-5, meaning the defensive tackle stops the fullback, the cornerman blitzes and is assigned to get the quarterback, while the defensive end is coached to stop the potential pitch out.

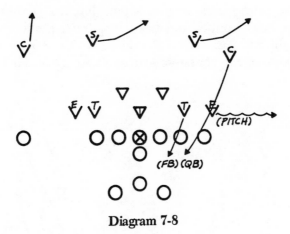

Diagram 7-8

Triple Option Versus Double Coverage

When running the Triple Option to the side of double coverage, the offensive quarterback must first think "keep," if the defense shuts off the fullback's dive and the double covering linebacker anchors in his double covering position. If the defensive end is coached to stop the fullback's dive and the double covering linebacker is taught to tackle the quarterback, there is no way the double teaming linebacker is able to get back to the inside if he is chugging the split end. Thus, the quarterback executes the keeper right after shuffling past the first key. (Diagram 7-9.)

If the double teamming linebacker begins to sprint in toward the ball just prior to the snap of the ball, so he would be in good position

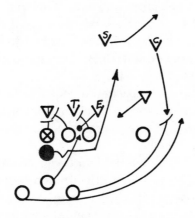

Diagram 7-9

to tackle the quarterback on the keeper play, the quarterback would simply carry out his option and make the pitch to the trailing halfback, with the split end running off the deep one third area and the lead halfback blocking the containing cornerback. (Diagram 7-10.)

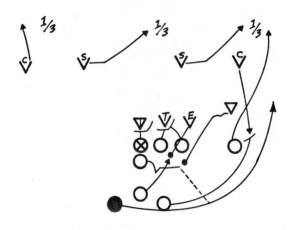

Diagram 7-10

Triple Option "Crack" Call

The word "crack" added to the Triple Option play calls for the split end to the side of the attack to execute a crack back block on the inside strong safety, while the lead halfback now is assigned to use his chop block on the isolated cornerback. Actually "crack" blocking to the split end's side is no more than an exchange of assignments between the cornerback and safetyman. The split end who is the crack blocker is taught to crack back on the second deep defender to the inside and the lead halfback is now coached to lead the trailing halfback around the corner and block the defender in the deep outside one third area. (Diagram 7-11.)

The lead halfback is coached to look for the second deep defender to the inside and anticipate blocking the containing cornerback, as long as the split end is able to crack back on the #2 defender (inside safety). (Diagram 7-11.)

The "crack" call is off if the four deep secondary decides to roll or rotate toward the flow. When this rotation occurs, the cracking split end is coached to begin his crack course toward the inside safetyman. If the inside #2 defender (safety) begins to rotate to the deep outside one third area, the cracking split end is coached to redirect his course

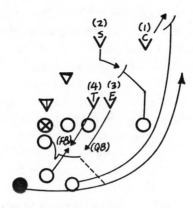

Diagram 7-11

and block his one third area. The lead halfback checks the inside safetyman; and if he sees the safetyman going to the deep one third area, he must now block the cornerman who is rolling up to his contain position. (Diagram 7-12.)

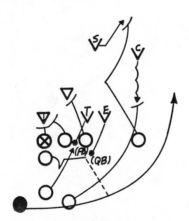

Diagram 7-12

If "crack" is called to the tight end's side, the tight end is assigned to block just the same assignment as the split end. This means the tight end looks for the inside safetyman to run an invert course and attempt to contain the pitch out from an inside-out angle. Thus, the tight end blocks the safetyman to his side before the deep defender is able to make the cut off approach. The lead halfback checks the

#2 defender (second deep defender to the inside) and blocks the cornerback, who is assigned the deep one third area, as soon as he realizes the tight end has blocked the strong side safetyman. Diagram 7-13 illustrates a well blocked corner for the ball carrier to make a break away on the pitch out. Since the backside trailing halfback is coached to ride the lead halfback's outside hip, a successful block by the lead halfback assures the offensive of a big play.

If the defensive four deep uses a rotating or rolling secondary action, the tight end uses the same blocking method as the split end and blocks the strong safety if he is assigned to defend the deep outside one third zone. (Diagram 7-12.) Diagram 7-13 pictures the inside safetyman rotating to the deep outside one third area so the tight end changes his approach and takes a wider angle so he will be able to block the safetyman who is retreating to the deep outside one third area. The lead back checks the inside safetyman; and once he realizes the strong safety is taking the deep outside area, he looks up the cornerback who is assigned to contain the potential pitch out. This is the defender the lead back blocks.

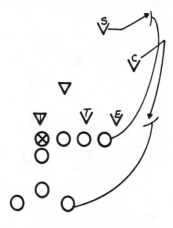

Diagram 7-13

CHAPTER EIGHT

The Drive Play

The drive play is a predetermined give to the fullback or the backside halfback. This play is an excellent play in the Triple Option series because its blocking assignments and technique, along with the dive fake to the fullback, almost mirror the dive execution of the Triple Option.

The important coaching points behind the success of the drive play are: (1) speed, (2) deception, and (3) execution.

Speed: Whether the quarterback calls the dive or the give to the second back, the speed at which the play hits is essential to its ultimate success. As soon as the first defensive key closes down to tackle the dive back, the frontside halfback blocks the defensive #2 defender the way he wants to go to the inside. This is a screen block when the frontside halfback is coached to gain position first and then fire out into the defender. (Diagram 8-1.)

Deception: The dive back must take an angular course where he hits as close off the fullback's tail as possible. The first fake to the diving fullback sets up the defense for the quick deceptive hand off to the double dive back.

Execution: Just as in all Triple Option series plays executed by the quarterback, running backs and blockers must reach near perfection. The relative motion (riding the back with the ball in the line of scrimmage) helps to minimize the chances of fumbling. On this double drive series, the quarterback has predetermined the ball carrier in the huddle; therefore, he is able to focus his eyes on the pocket targets of each diving back.

The blocking in Diagram 8-1 is exactly the same as the Triple Option blocking assignments for six of the seven offensive blockers. The one exception is the tight end who turns out on the outside defender. Thus, there is very little now in coaching points to add to the Drive series, to the previously installed Triple Option play.

Frontside Halfback

The frontside halfback's route may vary depending upon the reaction by the first defensive key. In Diagram 8-1 the lead back is coached to block the #2 defender with his outside shoulder (right). The reasoning behind this blocking technique is that the frontside halfback gets his head in between the defender and the ball carrier.

If the lead back aims for the #2 defender with his right shoulder, he is able to turn the defender to the outside (screen block) if the #2 defender steps across the line of scrimmage. (Diagram 8-2.) Thus, the blocker only has to get his body between the defender and the ball carrier, because he is taught to maintain position first and fire blocking power second.

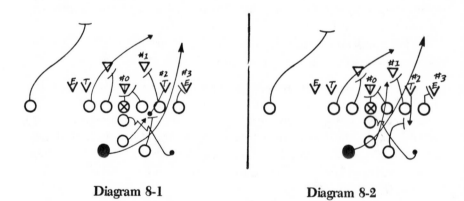

Diagram 8-1   Diagram 8-2

Coaching Point: While our coaching staff teaches the lead back to drive the #2 defender directly away from the hole with an aggressive fire out block, it is essentially a screen block.

Fullback

The fullback's assignment is essentially the same as his dive assignment on the Triple Option play, except the fullback is coached to dive directly over the back of the frontside guard's original position. The fullback must be careful not to cut back over the center, because this course may hold up the quarterback's hand off to the second diving backside halfback.

The fullback is coached to drop his outside shoulder after accepting the fake by the quarterback. The dip of the outside shoulder tends to draw the outside defenders toward the diving fullback. While this outside shoulder dip may expose the fake to the interior defenders, the wall off blocking technique set up by the center, frontside guard, and tackle walls off these interior defenders opening up the dive lane or crease discussed previously in the Triple Option coaching points.

The dive man should continue to carry out his fake and then use a cut off block on any inside pursuing defender who may have averted the wall off blocking assignments of the interior blocking linemen.

Ball Carrier

The backside halfback should cut as close off the fullback's tail as possible. Speed is essentaial for the success of a long gainer. The runner should accept the ball with his inside elbow high and hit the line of scrimmage at full speed with his shoulders parallel to the line of scrimmage. If his shoulders are parallel to the goal line, he will be able to drive through any arm tackles and be able to make an advantageous cut to his left or right as soon as he is past the line of scrimmage. The ball carrier should hold the ball in two hands and use an exaggerated body lean to make a hole, even if a hole does not exist.

Quarterback

The quarterback should take a quick 45 degree step with the lead foot and place the ball into the fullback's pocket. His second step should be a drag position step, which allows the quarterback to ride the fullback toward the line of scrimmage. The second step places the ball handler's shoulders parallel to the sidelines. After pulling the ball out of the fullback's pocket, the ball handler is coached to pull the ball back into his third hand (stomach) with two hands. Next, the quarterback takes a short second step with the right foot and places the ball into the backside halfback's pocket. The quarterback takes a second adjustment step with the left foot. He is coached to ride the ball into the halfback's pocket.

After handing the ball off to the second back, the quarterback is coached to drop back, setting up for a pass behind the offensive tackle's original position. As soon as he reaches his target area, he sets up and fakes like he is going to throw a pass.

The reader may question the coaching assignment of sending a smaller halfback to block a larger defending tackle; yet, the coaching assignment for the lead back is to screen block the defender any way he wants to go. This means the blocker should block the defender in the direction he wants to move. Thus, the frontside halfback's block is nothing more than screening the defender away from the ultimate ball carrier. The fake to the fullback usually sets up this block for the lead back. (Diagram 8-1.)

If the #2 defender steps across the line of scrimmage, the lead back is coached to block the defender to the outside with his outside shoulder; again, this is nothing more than a screen block by the frontside halfback.

All of the offensive linemen carry out their same blocking assignments in Diagram 8-2 as previously illustrated in Diagram 8-1. Only in Diagram 8-2, the ball carrier cuts inside of the frontside halfback's kick out block.

When running the drive play for maximum blocking power, we use three double team blocks by the offensive linemen to the point of the attack. The double team blocks are predicated upon the most aggressive or most difficult defender to handle on a one-on-one offensive block.

Red Call (Diagram 8-3)

If the middle guard is a quick moving or a particularly powerful defender, we use a double team block on the nose man. This double team block calls for the center to be the post blocker and the guard to be the drive blocker. (Diagram 8-3.) The lead back is coached to block the first defender outside of the double team block. The frontside tackle blocks #2 and the frontside end turns outside on #3. The diving fullback runs head on into the frontside defensive inside linebacker and helps to double team this defender with the lead back.

White Call (Diagram 8-4)

If the defensive linebacker is the strongest defender, a double team block may be featured against this defender. The guard becomes the post blocker and the frontside offensive tackle is assigned to drive block the linebacker. Again, the lead back blocks the first defender (#3 man).

Post and Drive Blocking Principles

All of the double team blocks are based upon the post man and drive man principle. The post man's assignment is to block the man over or block the first defender away from the point of the attack. The drive man's assignment is to drive down upon the first defender to the inside on or near the line of scrimmage. If no defender shows immediately, the drive man should continue to drive inside searching for a defender.

Therefore, these post and drive blocking principles hold up regardless whether the opposition stunts or stems to or away from the point of the attack. If the opposition jumps or changes the defensive alignment after the initial blocking call has been made, the offensive blocking linemen simply follow through their post drive rules.

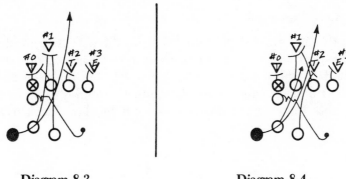

Diagram 8-3   Diagram 8-4

Red Call—Called Against An Okie Defense Jumped To A Gap Defense

Diagram 8-3 illustrates how the Red Call would have been blocked if the opposition stayed in the Oklahoma Defense. Once the defenders jump into a Split-Six gapped defense (Diagram 8-5), the Red Call would be blocked in the following manner. The center follows his assigned post blocking rule: No man over, block away from the point of the attack. Thus, he would drive block backside #1 defender. The frontside guard is the drive defender and would drive block #1 blocker in the inside gap. The frontside tackle would block the #3 man outside, and the tight end would turn out on the outside defender (#4 man). The lead halfback blocks the first defender outside of the drive block of the assigned drive man. He therefore blocks

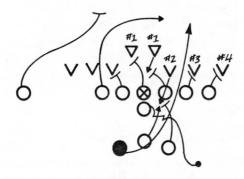

Diagram 8-5

the #2 defender any way he wants to go. Naturally, the #2 defender attempts to tackle the diving fullback, because he is the apparent ball carrier. As the defender steps to the inside, the lead back blocks him inside just the way he tries to go. (Diagram 8-5.) The center and tight end block their respective assignments.

Blue Call (Diagram 8-6)

If the offense wishes to double team the defensive tackle to the point of the attack, the center blocks #0, the frontside guard cuts off #1, the frontside offensive tackle posts #2, and the tight end posts #2. The frontside halfback blocks the first defender to the outside of the double team (#3) with an inside-out head-on block. (Diagram 8-6.)

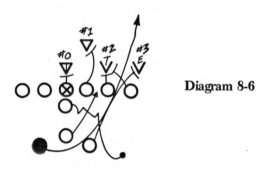

Diagram 8-6

White Call vs. 44 Defense (Diagram 8-7)

Against the 44 defense, the blocking call may feature a double team block by the guard and frontside tackle. The backside guard and offensive center reach block on the two inside linebackers. The lead blocks the first defender outside of the double team block. The tight end turns out on the first defender to his outside. (Diagram 8-7.) The frontside tackle drive block may actually develop into a combo block. This means that against the 44 defense, the tackle may play off his drive block and pick up the scrapping linebacker if the offensive guard can take the #2 man by himself. This is especially true if the #2 defender tries to pinch down to his inside into the #1 gap. (Diagram 8-8.) Thus, the post blocker drive blocks the defender who crosses his face, and the drive man adjusts his inside drive course to pick up the scrapping linebacker.

Gray Call (Fold Block) vs. The 44 Defense

The fold block is also used on the drive play where the offensive tackle blocks down on #2 and the offensive guard, toward the point of

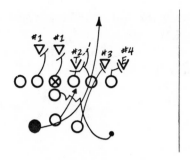

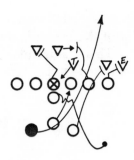

Diagram 8-7   Diagram 8-8

the attack, uses his step around assignment to pick up the scrapping frontside inside linebacker. All of the other blockers block their respective blocking assignments as illustrated in Diagram 8-9.

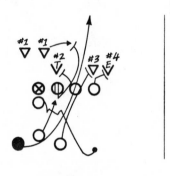

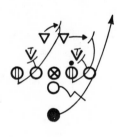

Diagram 8-9   Diagram 8-10

Double Fold Blocking Technique vs. 44 Defense

The double fold blocking technique is an excellent interior blocking call which helps to cut off the frontside inside scrapping linebacker. As well as the shuffling backside inside linebacker. If the two inside 44 linebackers decide to shoot the gaps between their respective #1 gaps (between the center and guard), the frontside guard sets, before he uses his folding step-around blocking technique. If the frontside guard sees the frontside inside linebacker shooting the gap, the blocker merely stays and blocks the blitzing linebacker. The offensive center sets, checking the backside linebacker, using a backside check step to guard against a backside linebacker's blitz.

If neither linebacker blitzes, the frontside guard uses his fold blocking technique to cut off the frontside linebacker. The backside offensive tackle scoops or folds toward the center and takes an angle to cut off the backside inside linebacker.

This is a fire blocking assignment for the fullback dive as well as the Triple Option play. (Diagram 8-10.)

CHAPTER NINE

The Drive Option

The reason this play series is referred to as the Drive Option is that the quarterback has the option to give the ball to the fullback if no defender attacks the fullback, or give the ball to the following backside halfback if the first defensive key decides to tackle the fullback. Thus, this Drive Option Series is actually a *Double* Drive Series.

While the Drive Option play was used successfully back in the early 1950's, the option technique in the drive series has made this play another explosion running series off the Wishbone Triple Option attack.

The Drive Option play is blocked just like the Triple Option by all of the offensive linemen when run to the split end side. When run to the tight end's side, only the tight end's blocking rule is changed. Therefore, the Drive Option Series is a most compatable play to the Triple Option series because the Drive Option series makes the Triple Option series go and vice versa.

The reason we refer to the Drive play as the Drive Option is that the quarterback options his first key exactly like the Triple Option. The quarterback's first key is the first defender who shows outside of the offensive tackle's block. This means that the quarterback focuses his eyes directly on this key as soon as he opens up to the side of the attack. The quarterback is coached to key this defender and to ride the fullback similar to the normal Triple Option play. If the first key takes the fullback, the quarterback is taught to pull the ball out of the fullback's pocket and give it to the slanting backside halfback, who is angling toward the point of the attack directly off the trail of the fullback. The quarterback's stance, steps, vision, and fake are exactly the same as in the Triple Option until he decides to keep the ball following the ride to the fullback. The lead halfback's rule, along with the backside halfback's assignment, is also adjusted differently from the Triple Option play.

Refer to Chapter 3 for the Quarterback's Optioning and Ball Handling Techniques.

Once the quarterback makes his decision to keep the ball, he is taught to take a slight adjustment step toward the backside halfback with his lead foot. This means the quarterback may have to enlarge his lead or open foot slightly if the backside halfback steps out too far outside of his prescribed course. Following the ride to the fullback, the quarterback must look directly at the backside halfback's pocket and place the ball directly into the halfback's pocket. Once the ball has been securely placed into the ball carrier's pocket, the quarterback is coached to drop back behind the original position of the playside tackle's position. As the quarterback drops back and sets up to fake throw, the fullback is taught to fake like he has the ball, covering up the fake by placing his two hands in a cup-like technique hiding the make-believe football in his stomach area. A good bend at the waist and the quarterback's swinging elbows make the defenders' rear view believe the quarterback actually has the ball and is dropping back for an apparent forward pass.

See Chapter 4 for the Fullback's Dive Techniques.

Frontside Halfback

The frontside halfback is coached to set a path directly at the first defender who shows outside of the offensive tackle's block. The reason we do not say the defensive tackle against the Oklahoma defense or the 52 defense is that the defensive end may pinch in and the playside defensive tackle may loop to the outside. (Diagram 9-1.) Thus, the frontside halfback should set a course for the first defender to *show* outside of the playside offensive tackle's block, who is the defensive end in Diagram 9-1. If the first key or first defender outside of the playside tackle attempts to stop or tackle the fullback, the frontside halfback is taught to pass up the first key and continue through the hole and look for the first inside defender to show. If no defender shows from the inside, the lead halfback is coached to block the first downfield defender directly in front of him. (Diagram 9-2.)

If the quarterback's first defensive key holds his position and does not attempt to tackle the quarterback, the frontside halfback is assigned to block this defender using his normal head-on blocking techniques. When the defensive key hangs on the line of scrimmage, the quarterback may decide to give the ball to the fullback on his normal dive route or fake to the fullback and give the ball to the backside halfback. We encourage the quarterback to give the ball to the second back on the Drive Series whenever the first key hangs on the line of scrimmage, because the lead halfback is taught to block the hanging defender. This block therefore opens up the hole at the point of the attack.

Diagram 9-1   Diagram 9-2

The frontside halfback is coached to look to the inside if the first key or #3 man (Diagram 9-3) tackles the fullback. The first inside man usually is the linebacker or possibly the safetyman.

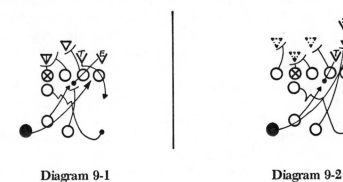

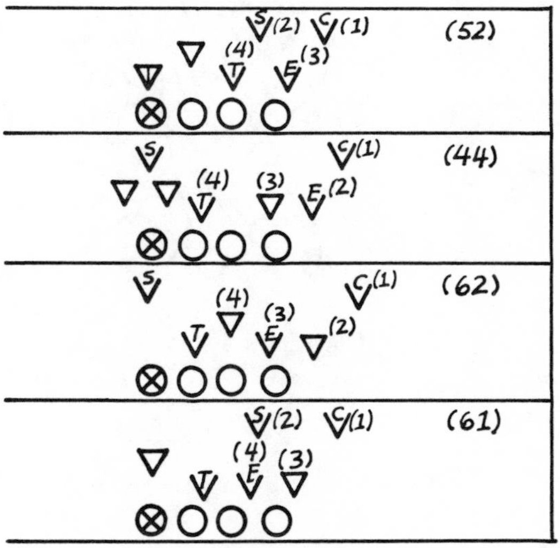

Diagram 9-3

Backside Halfback

The backside halfback takes a lead step with his frontside foot and then a cross over step with the back foot. On approximately the third step, the backside halfback should be ready to accept the quarterback's fake or the actual hand off. The outside foot should be forward with the inside foot to the rear.

Running the Drive Option versus an even defense, the quarterback is coached to option the #3 defender. If the #3 man attacks the fullback, the quarterback gives the ball off to the second man through. If the #3 defender does not attack the fullback and steps straight across the line of scrimmage, the quarterback gives the ball to the first man through (fullback).

In Diagram 9-4 the quarterback fakes the ball off to the fullback because the #3 defender is assigned to stop the fullback. The ball handler then hands the ball off to the backside halfback. The lead halfback sprints through the hole and blocks the first man downfield. In this instance, it is the deep middle safetyman.

The frontside guard and tackle execute the fold block to seal off the "crease." The backside guard and tackle use a fold block to eliminate the backside tackle and backside #1 linebacker.

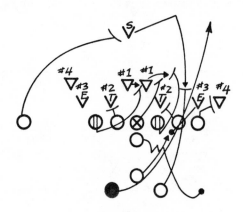

Diagram 9-4

CHAPTER TEN

How and When to Run

the Triple Option Counter Plays

First: The quarterback is taught to run the counter plays basically against an Eagle defensive alignment. (Diagram 10-1.) The alignment of the defensive tackle, on the outside shoulder of the offensive guard, makes the trap block easy by the backside pulling guard. This block gives the blocker a good inside-out angle on the defensive Eagle tackle.

Diagram 10-1

Second: Counter plays are good against defenses which feature quick scrapping or scalloping linebackers like the Oklahoma (52) and the 44 defenses.

Third: Counter maneuvers are successful against the Oklahoma defense when the defensive tackles freeze or hold their positions, attempting to read the first defensive key of the Triple Option. The freezing or holding techniques by the defensive tackles force the inside 52 linebackers to defend a greater lateral area against the counter action plays.

Fourth: Quick hitting counter plays off the Triple Option are particularly good versus stemming or stunting defenses. Often the countering ball carrier breaks away for a long gainer with minimum line blocking success, by merely running past the surprised defenders.

Fifth: Counter plays give the offensive blockers an advantage over fast flowing defensive linemen, because it allows the offensive linemen a chance to get good blocking position on their defensive opponents. Once the defenders momentarily move with the backs' stutter steps and the fake of the dive man, the defender is in a vulnerable defensive position. The success of the initial fake on the counter is a most important facet of breaking away from the long gainer off the counter play.

Sixth: The counter maneuvers keep the defense from rapidly pursuing the normal Triple Option play. Both the Triple Option play, combined with a few counters, help to compliment each other by keeping the defense "honest."

Quarterback Counter

Whenever our Triple Option Wishbone attack faces an opponent whose defensive linebackers are coached to key the running backs, the quarterback counter is an excellent play situation. The quarterback counter is a true counter, because all three of the set backs sprint away from the point of the attack. The halfback counter, discussed later in this chapter, send two potential running backs away from the point of the attack, while the third back (the ball carrier) takes one step away from the point of the attack and then cuts back toward the point of the attack. The quarterback counter not only draws the linebackers out of position, but also pulls the down defensive linemen away from the point of attack. This pull not only influences the defender away from the point of attack, but also helps to set up the offensive blocks on the moving defenders. The running backs' action, along with a good quarterback-fullback dive fake, places the defender in a poor defensive position. Just as he realizes he has been faked out of position, the offensive blocker blocks the surprised defender from the blind side.

The basic blocking rules for the quarterback counter are as follows:

Center	—	#0
Guards	—	#1
Tackles	—	#2
Tight End	—	Clear #3, Downfield

The defenders are numbered from the middle defender (#0) to the outside, with the closest defender to the middle defender being designated as #1, the next defender #2, etc. Against the Oklahoma defense, the middle guard would be #0, the inside linebackers would be #1, both tackles #2, and the defensive ends are #3.

The Oklahoma defense is numbered and blocked in the manner shown in Diagram 10-2.

The backfield action, illustrated in Diagram 10-2, is exactly the same action as the beginning of a Triple Option right play. All of the running backs carry out their respective assignments all through the play, and the quarterback is the only offensive back who breaks off opposite the backfield flow. The quarterback is coached to give the fullback a good ride and then pulls the ball out of the fullback's pocket at the last moment. The quarterback is taught to tuck the ball away into his stomach, with both hands, and push off his back right foot. On his first step, the quarterback is coached to key the center's block on the middle guard. If the middle guard breaks toward the flow off the backs, the ball carrier is then taught to cut off the center's block and run to daylight.

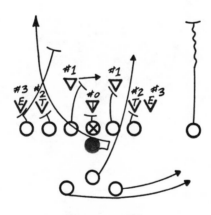

Diagram 10-2

The defensive draw of the counter and the fine blocking angles of the offensive linemen often break the quarterback counter off for long gainers.

The offensive linemen's blocking rules are illustrated against the 61 or Pro 43 defense in Diagram 10-3.

The offensive center blocks the #0 defender (middle linebacker) and blocks the shuffling linebacker in the direction the defender wants to go. Both the offensive guards are assigned to block the #1 defenders. Against the 61 or Pro 43 defense, the #1 defenders are down linemen, whereas against the Oklahoma or 52 defense, the #1 defenders are linebackers. The right guard has an excellent angle on the left defensive tackle, and the flow of the offensive back helps to set up the right offensive guard's block. The left offensive guard has a fine angle on the right defensive tackle (#1). When the flow of the backs goes away from this defender, he usually tries to fight down inside the left offensive guard's position. Therefore, the offensive guard to the side of the attack is taught to use a head-on block, shooting his head into the middle of the defender's body. The blocker is coached to attempt to drive the defensive tackle initially off the line of scrimmage and to stick with the defender and block the defensive tackle in the direction the defender attempts to go. Therefore, the point of the attack may be between the middle linebacker (#0) and the right tackle (#1), or between the left tackle (#1) and the left defensive end (#2).

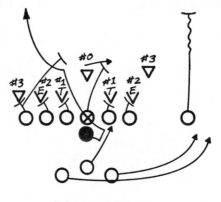

Diagram 10-3

The quarterback is taught to first key the center's block and then run for daylight. The offensive tackles both block their respective #2 defenders using their head-on block. The tight end is assigned to clear the #3 man and then block the right safetyman versus a box or two deep secondary, or the middle safetyman in a three deep secondary.

Against the 44 defense, there is no #0 defender. Therefore, the offensive center is assigned to check the #0 area for an apparent blitz over the #0 area by any one of the two middle linebackers. If no linebacker blitzes, the center is taught to block the #1 defender to the side of the attack. This moves up the left offensive guard's assignment to pick up the #2 defender. The left offensive tackle moves up his assignment by one and is assigned to turn on the #3 man. Both the offensive guard and tackle to the side of the attack have excellent blocking angles on their assigned defenders. The only difference between the two blockers' assignments is that the left guard blocks his defender (#2) before the left offensive tackle and must sustain his block longer, because he is the blocker at the point of the attack. The right guard's basic rule is to block #1, and the right offensive tackle's basic rule is to block #2; but against the 44 defense, these two backside offensive blockers are taught to exchange assignments. This means the right guard blocks #2 against the 44 defense, while the right offensive tackle blocks #1 versus the 44 defense. (Diagram 10-4.) The switch in blocking assignments is a necessity to give both of these backside linemen excellent blocking angles on the defenders. The right offensive tackle actually pulls to his left, just like a pulling guard's technique. The backside tackle is then taught to swing inside the right guard's blocks, with his shoulders parallel to the line of scrimmage as he turns upfield, and pick up the left inside 44 linebacker. The pulling tackle's shoulders must be parallel to the line of scrimmage in the event the defender may recover quickly and meet the blocker just as the pulling tackle turns upfield.

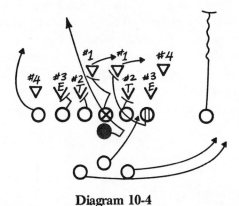

Diagram 10-4

If the 44 defense has an exceptionally strong defensive tackle to the point of the attack, the center may call for the defensive guard and tackle to double team block this #2 defender. (Diagram 10-5.)

This means the backside linemen block their basic assignments, and the offensive center blocks the playside or frontside inside linebacker (#1). The left tackle posts the defensive tackle at the point of the attack, and the left tackle is the drive man on the double team block. The double team blockers are taught to drive the #2 defender straight backward in order to make the inside frontside linebacker take a deeper and wider pursuit angle to attack the ball carrier. The left end is coached to use a turn out block on the linebacker in front of the defender.

The ball carrying quarterback fakes the ball to the fullback and then takes his counter route, which brings the ball carrier outside the double team block. The quarterback is taught to hug the double team block, because the left end has a most difficult block on the #3 linebacker.

Halfback Counter

With the continual pressure of the wide Triple Option threat, the inside defensive linebackers often become overly protective of this wide break away threat. The halfback counter play keeps these inside defensive linebackers honest by faking these linebackers one way and then countering with a handback to the opposite direction. The halfback counter play threat also helps to force the inside linebackers to stay at home when run successfully.

The halfback counter's backfield action starts out just like the Triple Option. Diagram 10-6 illustrates the right halfback flaring to the outside, just as he normally does on his routine Triple Option course. The fullback also sets course for his crease target, and the backside (left) halfback takes a stutter or set step to his right and then breaks for the left guard's inside foot. The quarterback steps to his right with his lead right foot on a 45 degree angle, as if he is beginning to run the Triple Option to the right side of the line of scrimmage. The quarterback then uses a short cross over step with his backside (left) foot to the right side. As soon as this left foot hits the ground, the

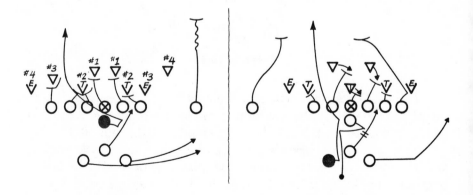

Diagram 10-5   Diagram 10-6

quarterback is coached to transfer all of his weight on the left foot and then step back with his right foot in the opposite direction. As the quarterback reverses his direction, his back is to the line of scrimmage. The ball handler is taught to push off his left foot and step with the right foot to give the ball to the diving left halfback.

There is no actual fake to the fullback on the quarterback's first directional movement, because the fullback's dive is a threat enough to make the defensive inside linebacker's move toward the side of the apparent dive keep or pitch threat. The quarterback steps back with his right foot toward the side of the point of the attack and may have to drag his left foot under him to gain the correct hand over balance as he slides the ball into the countering left halfback's pocket.

The left halfback shoots for the left guard's inside foot and focuses his eyes on the defensive middle guard. If the defender has moved toward the fullback's fake, the center has excellent position on this defender, and then the ball carrier is coached to look for the left guard's block on the playside inside linebacker. If the playside defensive linebacker has moved toward the first fake, the ball carrier will then break for daylight between the offensive left guard's block on the playside linebacker and the offensive left tackle's head-on block on the defensive right tackle. (Diagram 10-6.)

Another way of blocking the Oklahoma 52 defense is to have both the offensive guards and the offensive tackles switch their respective blocking assignments. This particular blocking scheme calls for the left offensive tackle to turn out and block the defensive tackle at the point of the attack. The left offensive tackle then delays, to allow the left guard to fire in front of him, and then loops up to the inside to block the right defensive inside linebacker. The initial fake to the fullback causes this linebacker to move in the direction of the fullback's fake. This allows the "scooping" tackle an excellent outside-in blocking angle on the shuffling inside linebacker. (Diagram 10-7.)

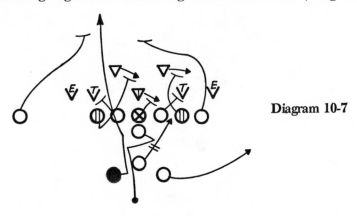

Diagram 10-7

The offensive center uses the same blocking technique as he used in Diagram 10-6.

The right offensive guard has a fine blocking angle on the backside offensive tackle guard simply needs a screen block on this defender who is farther out of position following the fullback's dive fake. The left offensive tackle takes a stutter step with his outside foot, to allow the right offensive guard to go in front of him, and then "scoops" to his inside to block the inside Oklahoma linebacker to his side. The right tackle sets a course which should take him to a position between the ball carrier and the left inside linebacker. The quick fake dive should influence the linebacker's movement slightly, but the blocking right tackle should be ready to use a head-on block on the redirected inside Oklahoma linebacker. All of the other blockers use their same assignments as illustrated in Diagram 10-6.

Against the 44 defense (Diagram 10-8), the playside offensive tackle and guard actually exchange assignments compared to their respective blocking assignments versus the Oklahoma (52) defense. The offensive guard turns out and blocks the right defensive tackle versus the 44 defense, while the offensive left tackle blocks the right inside linebacker across the point of the attack. The left offensive tackle's block is aided by the fake of the fullback's dive, and the blocking left tackle only has to drive block the linebacker in the same direction he is pursuing. The offensive center blocks the left inside linebacker. The defensive left linebacker is set up for the head-on block by the quarterback's apparent give to the diving fullback. The offensive right guard and tackle turn out on the defenders to their outside. The tight end blocks the deep middle one third area. The split end is assigned to block the deep defender to his side.

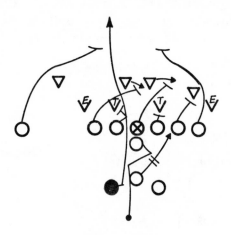

Diagram 10-8

The 61 defense is blocked similar to the Oklahoma defense (Diagram 10-6), only the center is now assigned to block the middle linebacker. The fullback's dive fake has more of a draw on the middle linebacker than it does on the middle guard; but this does not simplify the center's block on the middle linebacker, because this defender is deeper than the nose defender and has greater quickness, sight, and recovery time than has the middle guard in his four point stance. Thus, the center must get his head quickly between the middle linebacker and the point of the attack. Both of the offensive guards are responsible to turn out on the defenders on their outside shoulders. The offensive tackles have the same blocking assignments as the offensive guards. (Diagram 10-9.) The ball carrier attempts to run outside of the offensive guard's block, there is a strong possibility the defensive end (to the split end's side) has a fine chance of tackling the countering ball carrier.

Against the even (62) defense, we coach the countering ball carrier to cut inside of the playside (left) guard and center's double team block. (Diagram 10-10.) Therefore against many even defenses, the point of the attack may be directly over the offensive center's original position. Diagram 10-10 illustrates the left guard and center double teamming the defensive right tackle who is lined up on the nose of the offensive left guard. The left offensive tackle must shoot out quickly to get his head in front of the right inside 62 linebacker. This is one of the playside tackle's more difficult blocks, because the defensive linebacker is moving toward the ball carrier beginning with the first fake to the diving fullback. Once the blocking left offensive tackle gets his head in front of the pursuing linebacker, he may have to continue to scramble on all fours. We coach the tackle to scramble on all fours into the linebacker's legs and attempt to block the linebacker upfield and then continue to swing the blocker's tail in the progression of the

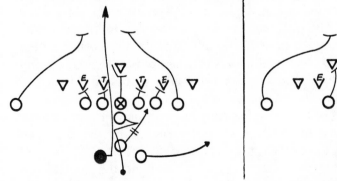

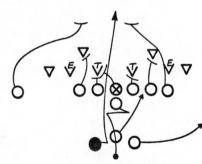

Diagram 10-9   **Diagram 10-10**

ball carrier. Both the backside offensive guard and tackle turn out on their respective defenders similar to the 61 defense. (Diagram 10-9.)

The Counter Option

The counter option play sets up the defense by instructing all four backs to make a quick stutter step in the opposite direction of the actual point of attack.

The quarterback is coached to key the #3 defender and make his pitch or keep, depending how this defender reacts to the quarterback. We coach this play as a pitch first, and the quarterback keeps the ball only when the defense has definitely taken away the pitchout.

All the backs take a quick parallel step in one direction and then shift their weight to the opposite foot and take off in the opposite direction. Along with the stutter step, the backs are also taught to use a head and shoulder fake in the same direction as the stutter step. This fake should help to freeze the defensive linebacker; therefore, the fake must be well executed. The stutter or set step should be parallel to the line of scrimmage so the defenders are held up or actually force the defenders to take a set step in the same direction as the offensive backs. Once the offensive backs have started in the direction of the point of the attack, it is hoped that the offensive blockers have achieved an advantageous blocking angle on their respective defensive blocking assignments. The defenders that are usually influenced the most are the defenders in a two point stance (ends and linebackers), because many of these defenders are keying the movement of the offensive backs.

The frontside back should make his quick stutter step and then set a dive course between the seam of the frontside guard and tackle. The offensive fullback makes a stutter step to his right and then sets off on a parallel course toward the left end. The fullback must be prepared to block the defender who is responsible for the pitch out —the #2 defender in both the Oklahoma (Diagram 10-11) 44 defense (Diagram 10-12). The pitchman takes a parallel step to his right then sets off on a parallel course to his left, to turn the corner of the defensive right end. The pitchman is coached to ride the outside hip of the leading fullback and stay to the outside, unless he is forced to cut up inside of the containing defender.

The counter option play is basically blocked man on man with the quarterback making his pitch or keep determined by the defensive play of the #3 defender. (Diagrams 10-11 and 10-12.)

Against the Oklahoma defense, the center and the frontside offensive guard block the defender over them. The frontside tackle blocks the defensive tackle, which isolates the defensive end (#3 man). This defensive #3 man is the defender the quarterback is coached to option off. As stated previously, the play is a pitch out first, and a keeper by the quarterback only if the defensive end forces the quarterback to keep the ball by attacking the possible pitch out.

Once the quarterback decides to keep the ball, he should cut on a 90 degree angle pushing off his back foot, dipping his inside shoulder, and placing the ball under both hands. The quarterback is now taught to drive for a minimum of five yards and then make his break after he has gained his five. Thus, the quarterback would cut up inside of the defensive Oklahoma end. (Diagram 10-11.)

When attacking the 44 defense, the frontside offensive guard and tackle execute a fold or step around block. (Diagram 10-12.) This features a quick drive block from an outside-in angle by the left tackle and a delayed fold blocking technique by the offensive right guard. No blockers block the two outside defenders on the line of scrimmage, because these defenders are usually assigned to stop the quarterback keep or the wide pitch out maneuver. If the quarterback is forced to keep the ball, he is taught to make it a quick keeper inside of the outside linebacker. A maximum split by the tight end often widens this head up linebacker and gives the quarterback more time to make up his offensive pitch or keep decision. It also gives the outside linebacker a greater area to defend against the outside option maneuver.

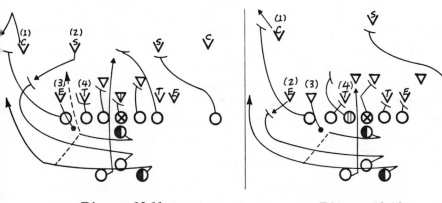

Diagram 10-11   **Diagram 10-12**

CHAPTER ELEVEN

Wishbone's Action Passes

Wishbone's Basic Action Pass Patterns

Since the split end is the basic pass receiver in the Wishbone formation, we teach him six baisc cuts: (1) Sideline, (2) Flag, (3) Deep, (4) Post, (5) Curl, and (6) Drag. Whenever the split or short side halfback is called into pass patterns, he runs a counter pattern so he will not run into the same zone as the tight end with the exception of a flood pass route. (Diagram 11-1.)

When running an all out pass attack, the offense will usually break the Wishbone formation into a Half-Wishbone alignment. From this formation, the Wishbone attack can still fake the dive off the Triple Option series and still have a possibility of five potential receivers running an assortment of pass patterns. (Diagram 11-2.)

Running a basic Wishbone Pro formation to the right features a flanker back to the right, a split end left, and one-half Wishbone alignment. The flanker is given three basic cuts, the tight end two cuts, and the split end, fullback, and halfback one pass pattern each. Diagram 11-3 illustrates this Wishbone Pro Triple Option Right Pass.

Shifting From Wishbone To Pro Wishbone

There are some coaches, who, in some Wishbone formations, like to replace their fullback with a top pass receiver when they are pressed into breaking their basic Wishbone alignment. Placing the top receiver in the middle of the formation (fullback's position) just prior to the snap of the ball allows the primary receiver to shift to either side of the formation. This one man shift gives the basic Wishbone a Split Pro Look, Split Slot Look, Split Wing Look, etc. (Diagram 11-4.)

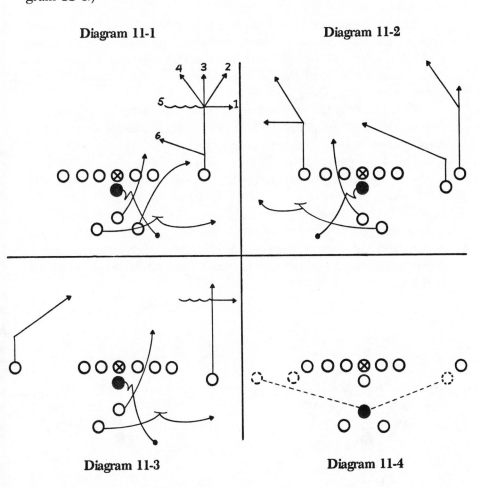

Diagram 11-1

Diagram 11-2

Diagram 11-3

Diagram 11-4

The Drive Pass

The Drive Pass to the tight end side is one of the most consistent passes to the strong side of the formation. This pass is particularly effective whenever a running play is expected. The double ride fake tends to hold the defensive linebackers and secondary defenders just long enough to break the receivers into the clear.

Both the receivers to the playside are in the same line of fire for the passer. This means the passer does not have to turn his head to pick up either receiver, because both the flat and flag patterns are in a straight line of vision.

In the event both of these receivers are covered, the fullback is coached to run a hook at ten yards deep, hooking in an area directly behind the original position between the playside offensive guard-tackle area.

The split end is coached to run a post pattern, and this backside receiver is often open for the long bomb because of the quick rotation of the secondary. If the split end is able to hit the seam between the deep middle zone and the backside deep one third area, the long gainer is assured. (Diagram 11-5.)

The frontside linemen use fire out blocking which simulates the running drive series, while the backside guard and tackle drop back to their wall off pass protection blocking techniques. (Diagram 11-5.)

The drive pass to the split end's side simply tells the split end to take over the tight end's assignment and the tight end runs the split end's assignment as in Diagram 11-1. The lead halfback runs a flat pattern; but, if the right cornerback levels off into the flat, the halfback is coached to run a more arrow-like pass pattern so he will gain ground and get open in between the playside safetyman's deep outside one third area and the corner back's level off flat zone. (Diagram 11-6.)

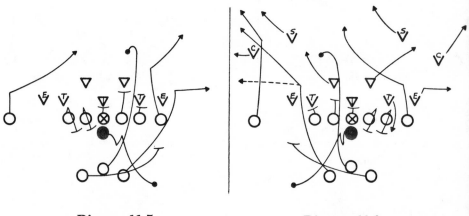

Diagram 11-5   Diagram 11-6

The quarterback sets up directly behind the original position of the frontside tackle. The backside faking halfback is taught to make the second ride fake and then take the correct angle to block the rushing defensive right end on a head-on course. The backside back is coached to block the rushing end low, to bring the rusher's arms down to protect against the halfback's low block. This enables the passer greater vision to hit the lead halfback or split end right now. (Diagram 11-6.)

Counter Option Pass

The Counter Option Pass is a quick pass usually to the tight end. There is a great amount of defensive draw on this particular play because the backs first draw the defenders in one direction and then counter step in the opposite direction. Just as the defensive linebackers are trying to recover and move laterally in the opposite direction of the offensive back's stutter steps, the passer hits the tight end with a quick pop pass. Naturally the pass is more successful when the option is run to the right with a right handed quarterback, but it can also be a success run to the left with a right handed passer. (Diagram 11-7.)

Diagram 11-7

The backfield counter fakes afford the tight end time enough to make his outside release and look over his inside shoulder for the quick pass. The passer must be coached to take something off the ball when throwing this quick pass so the quarterback does not knock the intended receiver's head off with a bullet-like pass.

The Counter Option Pass, just like the Wishbone Pop Pass, should be thrown between linebackers and never over the linebacker's head or the ball may take off into the deep defender's hands, or it may be deflected off the linebacker's raised arms, which may result in an interception.

The backside halfback runs a flair course just as the frontside halfback is coached to run on the Wishbone Pop Pass, since the backside halfback is the secondary receiver to the same side as the tight end. The passer is coached to throw this pass at the receiver's numbers, because a higher pass might be deflected off the potential receiver's fingers.

The fullback begins his parallel course then looks to block the first defender outside of the frontside offensive tackle's block. The fullback is taught to go after the defender and not to wait for the defensive rusher. The fullback is coached to throw low on the defender, just as the frontside offensive linemen's blocking technique, to bring the defender's arms down to ward off the blocker. Bringing the arms down low limits the chance of the defender's deflecting the quick low Pop Pass. (Diagram 11-7.)

Wishbone Pop Pass

The most consistent Wishbone pass over the years has to be the quick Pop Pass. The quarterback makes a quick fake to the fullback on his dive action fake and then raises up and quickly hits the split end running a short post route. The dive fake, along with the frontside linemen's fire out blocking, holds the defensive linebackers just long enough for the quarterback to hit his target just beyond the linebackers and in front of the deep secondary defenders. (Diagram 11-8.)

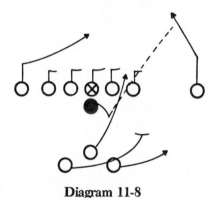

Diagram 11-8

This pass is also successful to the tight end. But when throwing the Pop Pass to the tight end, the end uses an outside release, just as he does in his normal Triple Option series, and then he looks to the inside for the quick pass.

The quarterback's passing technique is taught using the same first ride step back fake, with the frontside foot, to the fullback. Just as the fullback passes the quarterback, the passer straightens up, adjusts the back foot slightly and throws off his lead foot. The passer is coached to always throw between the linebackers and never over a linebacker. Whenever a passer attempts to throw over a linebacker, the defender always has a chance of getting a hand on the ball with a chance of deflecting the flight of the ball to another defender or the linebacker may make the interception himself.

If the passer finds the split end covered, the passer has a second option of leading the frontside halfback with the ball. The frontside halfback runs his parallel course just as he normally runs in his Triple Option series. Just as he is almost behind the split end's original position, the frontside halfback is coached to turn upfield and look for the ball over his inside shoulder. The pass receiver must give the passer a good target by opening up and making sure his inside shoulder does not get in the way of the ball. This flair type pass is almost a running play (as the passer usually hits the receiver behind the line of scrimmage) and ends up with a one-on-one challenge of the offensive halfback and a deep defensive back. The offensive back has the greater advantage over the defender, because he catches the pass turned upfield and has a chance to gain a great deal of forward momentum. (Diagram 11-8.)

The offensive linemen are coached to fire out low using their scramble blocking techniques on the defenders. This brings the defensive linemen's hands down low to ward off the low blocking offensive linemen. The low blocking technique keeps the defensive linemen's arms down low so they are unable to deflect the quarterback's quick bullet pass.

Counter Bomb Pass

The Counter Bomb Pass is run off the Wishbone counter running play fake. The double fake to the diving fullback and right halfback, the opposite directional draw by the left halfback route, combined with the quarterback's fake, helps to make this play a most productive scoring threat.

If for any reason the passer cannot throw the deep pass to the tight end on his post pattern, he can always dunk the ball off to his safety valve swinging left halfback. (Diagram 11-9.)

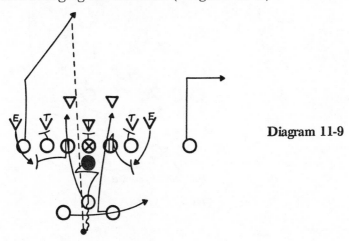

Diagram 11-9

Coaching Point: The real success of this play is the strong fake by the quarterback. Not only when faking the counter fakes, but when starting back toward his pocket, the quarterback is coached to place the ball on his inside hip (away from the defenders). As the quarterback places the ball on his hip, he is coached to actually walk backward for three to four steps, looking at the faking dive of the right halfback. The quarterback's bull-steps help to hold the deep back's attention just long enough for the tight end to hit the deep seam for the long bomb. Most quarterback's have the tendency to rush their last three or four steps; but, if they slow their drop back steps to a walk, the bomb will be a constant scoring play. Naturally this pass should be run on a definite running down, particularly in a short yardage situation right around the 50 yard line. (Diagram 11-9.)

Throwback Pass

Because of the current fashion of fast rotating defensive secondaries predicated upon the flow of the quarterback, the Throwback pass is a necessity for the long bomb and to keep the rotating secondaries honest. The most successful Throwback pass off the Wishbone sprint out passing series has proven to be the Throwback pass to the backside halfback toward the tight end's side.

Since most Sprint out passers favor throwing to the split end side off the Wishbone formation, the Throwback pass to the backside halfback has been a success, because the tight end's hook pass pattern tends to hold the fast rotating backside deep back just long enough for the backside halfback to swing back to the outside against the flow of the rotating secondary.

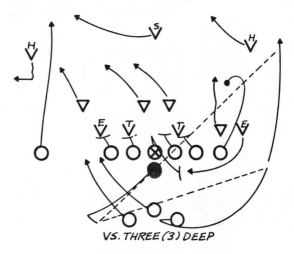

VS. THREE (3) DEEP

Diagram 11-10

Diagram 11-10 illustrates the Throwback pass against the three deep rotating secondary. With the backside halfback responsible to cover the deep two thirds zone area, it is impossible for this deep back to pick up the swinging backside halfback. The backside outside 44 linebacker is coached to cushion straight backwards to help defend some of the over burdened backside defensive halfback's wide two thirds zone. The hooking tight end helps to screen off or pick the outside linebacker's view of the swinging offensive halfback's pass pattern. Once the pass has been thrown, the tight end is in perfect position to block this defensive linebacker. (Diagram 11-10.)

The passer may hit the receiver just as he swings out of the backfield or throws deep to the halfback sprinting deep downfield. The depth of the pass depends upon the passer's protection and the rotation of the opposition's defensive backfield.

Throwing the Throwback pass against the four deep rotating defense is illustrated in Diagram 11-11. With a defender nose up on the center, the center blocks the #0 man, while the uncovered right guard sets and then blocks back on the rushing defensive left end. Again, the passer may wish to hit the swinging halfback quickly against the rotating four deep secondary.

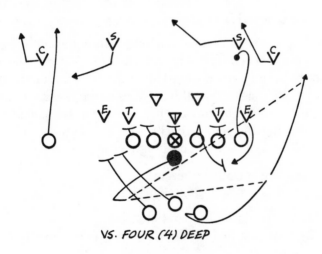

VS. FOUR (4) DEEP

Diagram 11-11

CHAPTER TWELVE

Coaching the "I" Triple Option
Backfield's Techniques

Utilizing The Quarterback Checklist Technique

The finest way to review coaching techniques with the quarter-back is to use a checklist teaching technique. Using a checklist, the coach can be sure he has covered all of the minute details and coaching points pertaining to the all important quarterback's Triple Option fundamentals and techniques. This Triple Option checklist can be used in studying the quarterback's performances on videotape and films as well as on-the-field coaching techniques.

Quarterback's Triple Option Checklist

A.   Stance and Body Position

1. Use confortable, parallel stance.
2. Feet should be placed comfortable, directly below the armpits.
3. Stance must be constant on all running and passing plays.
4. Knees should be bent comfortably.
5. The quarterback's body should be parallel to the center's stance. The quarterback's shoulders should be even and parallel to the center's hips.
6. Eyes should be trained straight ahead, looking the middle linebacker, middle guard, or safetyman right in the eye.

7. The weight should be evenly distributed on the balls of the feet.
8. The total stance should reflect the quarterback's poise and confidence.

B. Hand Position Prior to Snap

1. Top hand should be placed under the center's tail with the wrist placed one and one-half inches deep.
2. Pressure should be exerted upward by the top hand which gives the center the feel of a target.
3. Pressure helps to make the quarterback's hands follow through, riding the center forward.
4. The fingers should be spread in a relaxed manner.
5. The arms should be bent slightly and kept close to the body.
6. The top hand should "raise" the center's tail to the desired height.
7. The upper hand is the target and the clamp hand.
8. The bottom hand is used to trap the ball.
9. The lower hand's fingers should be spread slightly and extended perpendicular to the ground.
10. The bottom hand should be slightly forward, lower and to the side of the top hand.
11. The thumb should be placed parallel to the thumb of the top hand.
12. Trap ball immediately following the ball hitting into the top hand.
13. Lower hand should fold under the ball.

C. Cadence

1. Calls must be made in a loud, clear voice.
2. Cadence is a combination of rhythmic and non-rhythmic counts.
3. Quarterback only moves on snap of ball, not on snap number.
4. Cadence must reach near perfection for play timing.
5. All play callers must use same cadence on all signal calls.
6. Loud, sharp, and clear snap count helps to fire offense off the ball.
7. Quarterback's cadence should be used throughout practice sessions in all offensive drills.
8. Make sure all players are in down position before calling cadence.

D.   Snap Exchange

1. Ball should smack into quarterback's hand firmly.
2. Laces should be placed into the signal caller's top hand.
3. Ball should hit the groove of the top hand.
4. The ball should hit the top hand at a slight angle.
5. "Give" with the ball, by following through with the ball, riding the center forward on the snap.
6. Get the ball in both hands and pull it to the third hand (stomach).

E.   Receive Ball from Center

1. Adjust hands as pulling ball into stomach.
2. Keep elbows close to the body.
3. Crouch over the ball when it is in the third hand.
4. Keep the body between the ball and the defense.
5. Make ball adjustments with your hands while the ball is in your stomach.
6. Protect the football with your hands, arms, and torso.

F.   Mentally the Quarterback Must Check the Defense

1. First, he must read his dive key.
2. Second, he must read his pitch or keeper key.
3. Both of these keys are selected using peripheral vision.
4. The eyes control all of the quarterback's hand and eye movements.
5. Focus eyes on dive key as soon as the ball hits hands.
6. Think, "pitch," all the way.

G.   Ball Handling

1. Keep both hands on the ball.
2. Keep elbows in close to the body.
3. Reach back to begin dive ride.
4. Place the ball into the dive back's pocket.
5. Ride dive back smoothly, placing ball on dive back's far hip.
6. Extend arms fully.
7. Don't ride ball past belt buckle.
8. Quarterback—dive mesh must reach perfection.
9. If hand off—backside hand is last hand on ball.
10. If fake—pull ball out with both hands.
11. Put ball back in third hand (stomach).

H.   Footwork

1. Step with lead foot as center snap hits hand.

2. First step should be with lead foot on 45 degree angle.
3. Step back toward the dive back; don't overstep.
4. Ride begins on first step.
5. Second step is adjustment step.
6. Second step is an adjustment drag step.
7. Second step keeps quarterback close to line of scrimmage.
8. Step parallel down the line of scrimmage.
9. Hand off begins or ride ends on second step.
10. Give actually takes place before second step hits ground.
11. Length of adjustment step depends upon dive back's speed.
12. Adjustment step is made parallel to line of scrimmage.
13. Second step should be parallel to lead step.
14. Put weight on foot to eliminate false step.
15. Be ready to step around collision area.
16. Don't rush dive key.
17. If keeper—drive off back foot.
18. Sprint down the line of scrimmage to challenge second key.
19. Learn to pitch, running at full speed.
20. Step with same foot (toward target) as pitching hand.

I. Read First Key (Dive Key)

1. First key (dive key) is first defender outside of tackle's block.
2. Place the ball into dive pocket as you read dive key.
3. Hand ball to dive back, if first key steps across line.
4. Hand ball off to fullback if key is in #7 defensive position.
5. Keep ball if key attacks drive back.

J. Read Second Key (Keeper Key)

1. Challenge second key with shoulders parallel to sidelines.
2. If second key feathers (widens), run keeper.
3. If second key freezes (squats), run keeper.
4. If second key attacks, pitch the ball.
5. Be ready to pitch immediately after mesh to split end's side.

K. Ride Fake

1. Don't ride fake past quarterback's belt buckle.
2. During ride, quarterback's shoulders should be parallel to sidelines.
3. If trouble riding and reading first key, keep the ball.
4. Make sure dive back does not steal ball.

5. Pull the ball out as second step hits the ground.
6. Keep the body between the defender and dive back as much as possible.

L.   Keeper Play

1. Plant the back foot and push off.
2. Cover the ball with both hands.
3. Dip the inside shoulder.
4. Bend body over the ball to protect the ball.
5. Be ready to be hit immediately.
6. When in doubt, keep the ball.
7. Make your three and one half yards before cutting.

M.   Pitch Out

1. Adjust ball to chest prior to pitching.
2. Keep your eyes on the target area.
3. Think, "pitch," first and foremost.
4. Pitch with one hand, push-shot technique.
5. Pitch ball in flat trajectory.
6. Time the pitch out depending upon trail back's speed.
7. Pitch ball above trail back's waist.
8. Don't make pitchman slow down for pitch.
9. Step with same foot as pitching hand.
10. Pitch knuckle ball type pitch out.
11. Learn to pitch at full speed.
12. Pitch with right hand to right and vice-versa.
13. Don't pitch on second step after turning upfield.
14. Shoulders should be parallel to sidelines on pitch.
15. The best pitch out is usually chest height.
16. The faster the quarterback runs, the slower the pitch out.

N.   Absorbing Blow Following Pitch

1. Turn shoulders parallel to line of scrimmage.
2. Relax in fetal-like position.
3. Turn hips one quarter turn into defender.
4. Arm and shoulder may be used to ward off defender.
5. Be ready to be hit instantly after mesh to split side.

The reader is referred to Chapter 3—"How to Coach the Triple Optioning Quarterback," for a more in-depth review of specific quarterback coaching methods and techniques.

"I" Fullback's Stance and Alignment

The "I" fullback's stance, depth, and alignment has been covered in Chapter 4—"Triple Backfield Techniques." All of the fullback's assignments and techniques are similar to the Wishbone's coaching points as described and illustrated in Chapter 5.

"I" Tailback's Stance and Alignment

The tailback lines up directly behind the fullback with his heels 17 feet from the tip of the ball. The tailback is instructed to use a balanced two point stance with his hands resting comfortably on his knees. The tailback's weight should be evenly distributed so he can take off downfield or to his left or right.

The tailback is referred to as the pitchman, because he is the back who will receive the quarterback's pitch out on the third phase of the Triple Option.

The pitchman must take off with the same open step technique as used in the Wishbone and Veer formations. Since the tailback is lined up closer to the ultimate pitch out (behind the center as compared calculate his speed so he does not sprint too fast to a position beyond the four yard quarterback-tailback pitch out ratio.

The tailback's second step should be a cross over step on a parallel route which will take the "I" back to a position four yards outside and four yards deeper than the optioning quarterback. When running the Triple Option to the split end's side, the tailback should try to break outside of the end's reach block on the containing defender. A slight head and shoulder fake by the ball carrier can help to set up the tight end's reach block on the containing defender. This quick fake may draw the containing defender to the inside so the tight end may more successfully reach his head beyond the container's outside knee. (Diagram 12-1.) The flanker to the outside of the tight end is assigned

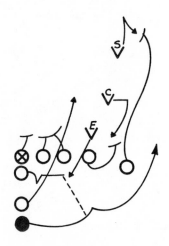

Diagram 12-1

to wall off the deep defender who is assigned to defend the deep outside one third area. Therefore, the ball carrier is taught to stay outside of the wide blocker's stalk block technique. (Diagram 12-1.)

If the two wide receivers exchange their assignments, the flanker back is assigned to block down upon the containing back, while the tight end is coached to swing around to the outside and employ the stalk block technique on the secondary defender assigned to defend the deep outside one third area. Using this exchanged blocking assignments, by the two widest offensive players to the strong side of the formation, the ball carrier is coached to keep as wide as possible running outside of the wall blocking technique of the tight end and flanker. (Diagram 12-2.) The ball carrier is taught to stay just on the outside hip of the tight end's outside swing blocking course.

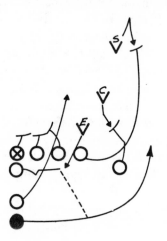

Diagram 12-2

CHAPTER THIRTEEN

How to Coach the "I" Triple Option

Advantages of Using The "I" Triple Option Attack

Some advantages of running the Triple Option off the "I" formation are:

The "I" set minimizes the coaching and practice hours spent on the field, because the tailback will be the primary pitch man while the fullback will be the dive back. This means the fastest back will be a constant threat to sweep the corner of either side of the offensive formation.

The "I" tailback is a pure runner; he does not have to spend a great deal of time blocking at the corner like the Wishbone halfbacks.

With the additional halfback employed as a flanker, wing, or slot back, the offensive formation tends to spread out the defense. It also gives the formation a more consistent passing attack then the basic Wishbone formation.

The tailback is in a closer position to turn the corner to either side of the formation than the Wishbone three back set. These few feet are often the inches needed to break away the pitch out, off the Triple, for the big play.

The quick threat of the "I" tailback turning the corner forces the defensive perimeter to show their defensive responsibilities immediately by alignment. Thus, the quarterback knows the defender who will be assigned to the fullback, quarterback, and pitch man, often prior to the snap of the ball.

The Triple Option features the best back (tailback) to sweep either corner and cuts down his practice time as a lead blocker and pass receiver.

The next best ball carrier goes in, if an injury occurs, as tailback and not necessarily at a particular left or right halfback position. Thus, it puts in the second best running back rather than the fourth best running back, substituting a specific back at right and left running backs respectively.

The "I" Triple Option attack solidifies the four-four yard relationship between the quarterback and the pitch man, because the quarterback is always pitching the ball to the same back. This allows the quarterback more practice time to read the one pitch man rather than the two potential pitch men using the Wishbone set.

The "I" backfield alignment helps to set up the quarterback's sprint out pass-run series. This is one of the finest pass-run options in football, and the fullback-tailback stack gives quick blocking support for the sprint out pass in either direction.

The Pro "I" formation helps to spread the opposition's defense with two wide receivers to both sides of the formation. The "I" backs (tailback and fullback), lined up in their stack alignment, is an excellent alignment for the sprint out pass. This formation is also a solid backfield set to run the sprint draw, or cut play.

The "I" set also gives the offense a strong interior running attack as the fullback is able to lead the tailback to the point of the attack from offensive tackle to offensive tackle.

"The "I" backfield set is also an excellent backfield alignment for an offensive shift of backs. The backs from the Pro "I" set can quickly shift into split backs, Power "I", or "I" slot formations.

"I" Triple Option Blocking Adjustments

Against the outstanding inside 52 linebacker, it may be necessary to double team the inside linebacker. The frontside guard is assigned to post block this defender, and the offensive frontside tackle is coached to double team this defender with his offensive teammate. Instead of driving directly at the linebacker (dotted line in Diagram 13-1), the tackle may be coached to go outside of the defensive tackle. (Diagram 13-1.) The coaching point behind this technique is the Oklahoma linebacker is coached to key the movement of the offensive tackle (even though he may be assigned a specific back to tackle versus a Triple Option play). This outside route to make the double team block on the inside linebacker often holds the defensive tackle, who is the quarterback's first key, just long enough for the ball handler to get a strong first read. If the defensive tackle steps out for the blocking tackle's outside route, the quarterback will simply hand the ball off to the fullback.

Although the frontside or playside tackle's assignment is exactly the same man, his path to the blocker may hold the defensive tackle just long enough to make the first phase of the Triple Option success-ful. The offensive tackle's outside route also cuts off the quick scrap-ping linebacker's inside-out pursuit from his defensive position.

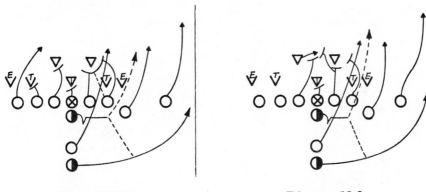

Diagram 13-1   Diagram 13-2

Another variation off the blocking pattern illustrated in Diagram 13-2 is teaching the posting frontside guard to post block the defen-sive linebacker to the point of the attack and then chug-off to cut off the backside linebackers. This blocking technique, versus the Ok-lahoma defense, cuts off both the frontside and the backside scrapping and scalloping linebackers. If the interior offensive blockers can seal off both 52 linebackers, one of the three Triple Option backs should be able to break loose for consistent gainers. (Diagram 13-2.)

Against the 44 defense both inside linebackers are cut off by the center, frontside guard and frontside tackle. Using this interior block-ing technique, our quarterback is instructed to pre-call the quarter-back keeper or the pitch out in the huddle. Since the fullback knows he is not going to get the ball and the frontside tackle is coached to seal off the split linebacker to the point of the attack, the fullback now uses a low chop block on the defensive tackle who is assigned to stop the fullback. We want the fullback to execute a chop block rather than just running into the defensive tackle, to the point of the attack, because we want this defender down and unable to spin off the full-back. (Diagram 13-3.)

If the defensive tackle and end attempt to pinch down to stop the dive and keep play, the offensive blockers at the point of the attack must be ready to pick up this stunt. (Diagram 13-4.)

The frontside guard is coached to pick up the pinching defensive tackle to the point of the attack. The offensive right tackle is coached to pick up the scrapping linebacker as soon as the defensive left tackle pinches down across the right offensive tackle's face. (Diagram 13-4.)

As soon as the quarterback makes his ride to the fullback, he must be ready to make the one handed pitch out as soon as possible, so that the pinching defensive #3 man is not able to disrupt the pitch out.

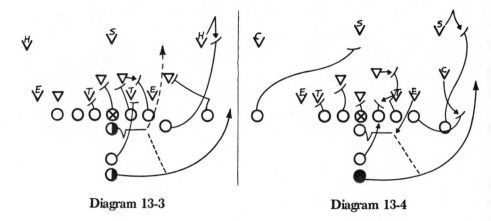

Diagram 13-3   Diagram 13-4

Triple "I" Versus Containing Rolling Cornerman

Against a fast rolling secondary, we often use the kick out blocking technique for the tight end. The tight end is called upon to kick out on the rolling cornerback whose assignment is to contain the pitch out maneuver.

If the tight end kicks out on the containing corner back, the tailback is coached to turn up inside of the kick out block. All of the other members of the offensive unit carry out their usual Triple Option blocking assignments. (Diagram 13-5.)

Double Coverage Versus The "I" Triple Option

Whenever we use three wide outs, we have found that many of our opponents want to use double coverage against our attack, expecting the offense to feature a strong passing attack. The offense likes to counter the double coverage of stationing a linebacker on one wide receiver to one side, a cornerback on one wide receiver to the other side, and a linebacker in a walk-away position toward the two man wide set, by automaticking the Triple Option away from the strong side of the formation.

Diagram 13-6 illustrates how many defenses will align their defense versus a wide slot one way and a split end to the opposite side. Since the defensive end to the split side must play contain versus the potential Triple Option pitch to his side, the offensive split tackle and guard double team the defensive right tackle. The center reach blocks the middle linebacker and the left tackle and guard double team block the defensive right tackle to open the crease for the quick give to the dive man. (Diagram 13-7.)

Attacking The Gap Eight Goal Line Defense With The Triple "I" Option

When attacking the Gap Eight defense, the quarterback must be ready to make his pitch quickly, because each defender is normally assigned to pinch to the inside from their gap alignments. (Diagram 13-8.)

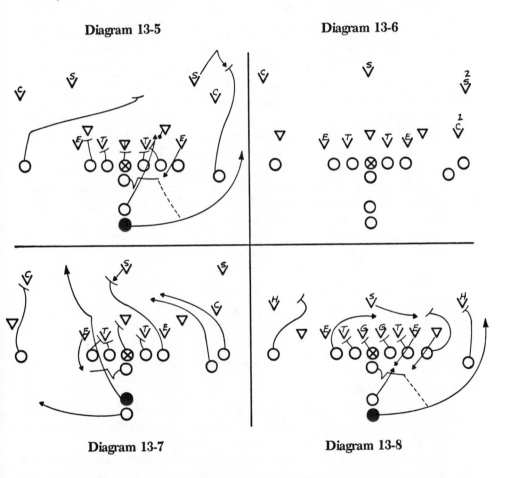

Diagram 13-5   Diagram 13-6

Diagram 13-7   Diagram 13-8

The fullback is coached to drive powerfully through the #3 defender if he does not get the ball, so that the fullback #3 defender's collision will not force the offensive quarterback to step off the line and belly around these two players. Forcing the quarterback to run around the first key collision area may throw off the four by four yard relationship between the quarterback-pitchman versus the second defensive key of the Triple Option.

Once the quarterback gets the pitch off, the ball carrier has free sailing because the flanker and the tight end have fine blocking angles on their respective men, and the ball carrier is able to turn the corner and almost walk into the end zone, in some instances.

The quarterback, who has been coached to get off a quick pitch out against any goal line defense, will continually put points on the score board for any Triple Option attack.

Fold Blocking

Since the Split-40 or 44 defense uses lateral movement by the big down defensive linemen to protect the inside linebackers, the fold block is taught to the offensive blockers. The defensive tackle in this defense (Diagram 13-9) is coached to fire down and through the offensive guards so the guards are unable to get out and block the inside linebackers. Therefore, we teach our guard and tackle toward the point of the attack to use a fold or step around block by blocking down with the offensive tackle on the defensive tackle. The defensive tackle is coached to take a minimum split, so that he can cut off the defensive tackle's penetration by keeping his head between the defender and the ball. The defensive guard then steps around to his right, keeping his shoulders parallel to the line of scrimmage, and looks to block the scrapping inside linebacker.

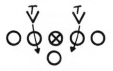

Diagram 13-9

The offensive guard's technique is to step with the frontside foot and place his arm on the offensive tackle's hip. The guard should keep his shoulders parallel to the line of scrimmage, to enable him to clear the offensive tackle. As soon as the offensive guard clears the tackle's block, he should look to the inside and pick up the scrapping frontside inside linebacker. Using this fold or step around blocking technique and fundamentals, the offensive guard is able to carry out his fold block blind folded because he actually executes his technique by feel as well as by sight. (Diagram 13-10.)

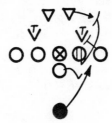

Diagram 13-10

The fold blocking technique forces the defense to designate a defender to attack the fullback on the Triple Option from an outside-in technique, because the frontside guard is able to seal off the crease with this block. If the playside end takes the quarterback and the outside linebacker is responsible to take the pitch man, the fullback has free sailing downfield. There is no way the inside linebacker can be expected to consistently tackle the fullback from an inside-out angle whenever a fold block has been called. (Diagram 13-11.)

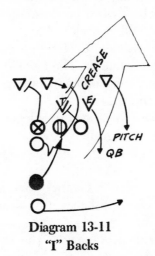

Diagram 13-11
"I" Backs

The offensive center insures against a straight-on blitz by the frontside linebacker blitzing into the center-guard gap by stepping with his frontside foot, checking for the potential blitz. As soon as the center sees the frontside inside linebacker scrape away toward the point of the attack, the center is coached to look up the backside inside linebacker.

Fold Versus 52 (Loose Linebacker)

The fold block is also executed against a loose playing Oklahoma or 52 linebacker. The frontside linebacker uses the same step around blocking technique as described versus the 44 defense. Against the Oklahoma defense, the offensive guard must take a slightly longer set step to make sure the inside frontside linebacker does not blitz straight over the guard's position.

The fold block is the best call whenever the offense anticipates a stunt between the defensive tackle and the frontside inside linebacker.

Head-On Block

The blocker is taught to take on the defender by exploding off the near foot, stepping directly at the defender with a wide balanced base. The blocker's back should be parallel to the ground and his eyes should be aimed directly at the defender's numbers. The blocker's head should be up and the neck should be in a fundamental bulled-neck position. Contact should be made with the blocker's forehand directly into the defender's numbers, and then he should whip the arms into the defender's stomach. The upward whip of the arms should be accompanied by rolling the hips upward on contact. Therefore, the blocker is hitting forward first and then upward after the initial explosion. The head must be maintained in an upward position aided by the blocker's bulled-neck technique. After the explosion, the blocker is coached to use short, choppy, machine gun-like steps to gain movement on the defender. The blocker must maintain his wide base, and a second and third effort will drive the defender backward and off the line of scrimmage.

The head-on block is taught by blocking large dummies over boards and under our cage-like covering. The boards keep the blocker's base wide and the ceiling-like cages force the blockers to stay low in a forward hitting technique.

The cage or chute drill is a competitive phase of blocking fundamentals, and the blocker must drive the dummy completely off the board. Later the dummy holder is allowed to attack the blocker on the snap count and put added pressure on the blocker. The board is also placed on a 45 degree angle to the blocker so he must drive the defensive dummy the entire length of the board.

The Scramble Block

The scramble blocker must fire out on the count and fire his head four inches above a moving defender's lead knee. If the blocker is unable to get his head in front of the pursuing defender, he is taught to fire his head in between the defender's legs. This scramble blocking technique, on all fours, chops down the defender.

This scramble blocking technique is used primarily on a down lineman. The chop block is used primarily on the shuffling defensive lineback.

The Playside Wide Receivers (Flanker or Split End)

The wide receivers are coached to sprint off the line of scrimmage and aim for a target area one yard outside of the secondary defender, who has been assigned to defend the deep outside one third area of the field. The wide receiver is taught to sprint just like he is running a deep up pass pattern to force the defensive back to defend the deepest part of his one third zone.

The wide receiver keeps sprinting until the defender breaks down, and the wide receiver is coached to break down as soon as the defensive back breaks down. The blocker is coached to maintain an outside and shallow position. This means the wide receiver maintains an outside position on the defender and a shallow position on the defensive back, which keeps the defender in front of the blocker. Therefore, the blocker keeps his body between the defender and the ball carrier. We do not want the blocker to leave his feet, because once the blocker overextends himself, he is lost. The blocker actually stacks or slow blocks the defensive back. (Diagram 13-12.)

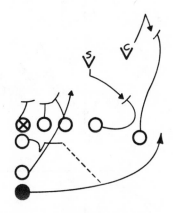

Diagram 13-12

If the defensive back attempts to attack the ball carrier by crossing the blocker's face, the blocker is told to stick his helmet into the middle of the defender and stay with him. The ball carrier is coached to cut off this block.

If the deep back attempts to break inside of the potential wide blocker, the wide man is coached to block the defender the way he wants to go. Therefore, the blocker merely blocks the defender to the inside, enabling the ball carrier to cut outside of this wall off block.

This block is referred to as an outside leverage block by the wide blocker.

The Backside Wide Receiver (Flanker or Split End)

The backside wide receiver is assigned to block the deep middle one third area. His block is referred to as an inside leverage block. The wide receiver runs his route just as he would be running a deep post pass pattern. The blocker is taught to sprint directly at the deep defender until the deep defender recognizes it is the Triple Option play. The blocker again sprints to the target area which puts him between the defender and the ball carrier.

The normal blocking pattern of the wide backside blockers end up forcing the secondary defender deep. As long as the blocker maintains his leverage on the defender, the ball carrier is free to advance

Diagram 13-13   **Diagram 13-14**

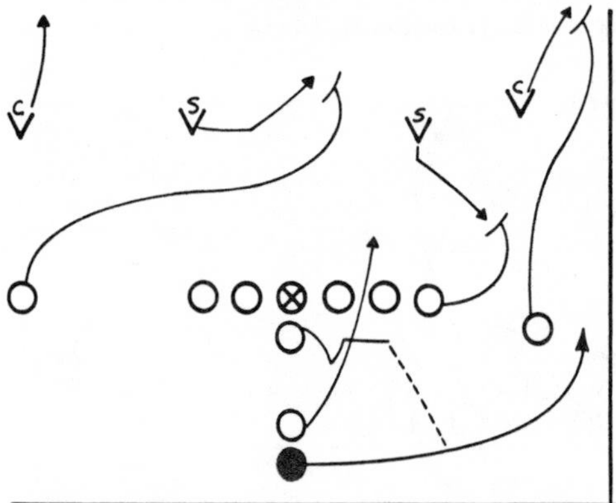

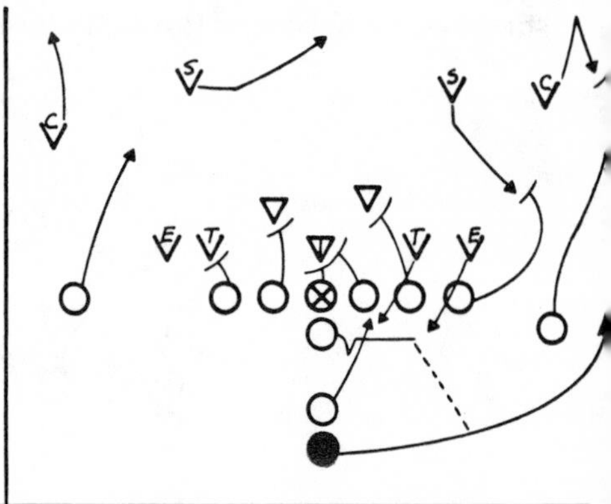

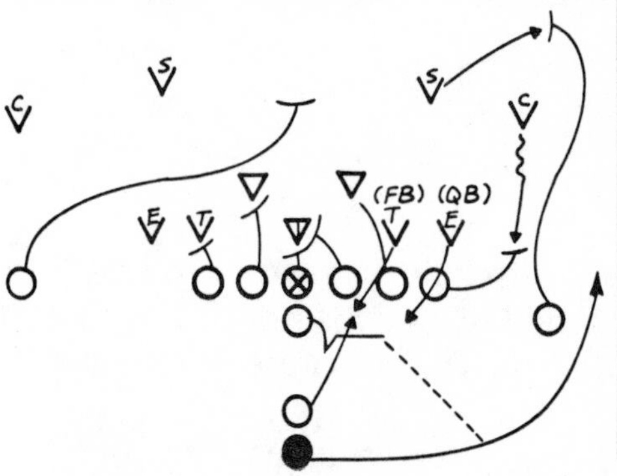

Diagram 13-15 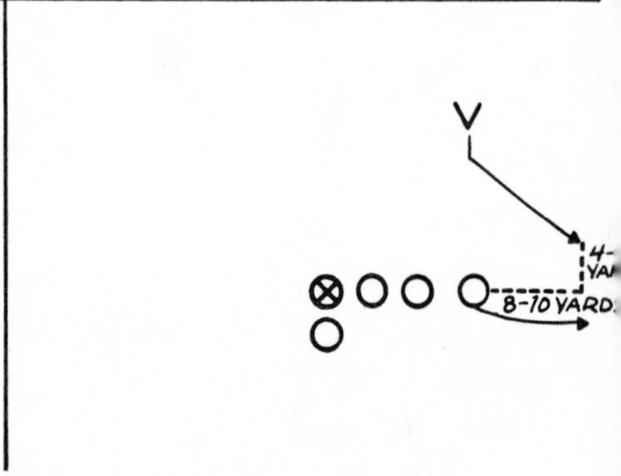   **Diagram 13-16**

with the wide backside receiver gives the blocker the proper blocking angle on the defender assigned to cover the deep middle one third zone. (Diagram 13-13.)

The Tight-End Triple-"I" Blocking

The tight end's assignment is to block the defender who is responsible for tackling the pitchman. The blocker's approach must be a flat lead step down the line of scrimmage attempting to gain width on the defender. By this third step, he should be able to read the defender who is responsible to stop the pitchman on the Triple Option.

Against the invert defender (Diagram 13-14), the strong side safetyman is responsible to defend against the pitchman (sweep). The tight end is coached to take a flat course along the line of scrimmage to a point where he will meet the strong safetyman to stop the potential pitch out. This target area is about eight to ten yards outside of the tight end's original position and four to six yards in depth. (Diagram 13-16.)

The tight end's coaching points are to sprint along the line of scrimmage and set a course for the target area. (Diagram 13-17.) The blocker should aim for the strong safetyman's outside knee and get his head outside of the defender. If the safetyman continues on his attack course, the blocker is coached to chop the defender's outside knee out from under under him to enable the pitchman to turn the corner and continue upfield.

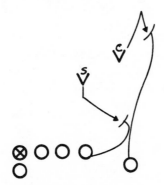

Diagram 13-17

If the strong safetyman attempts to run with the blocker to the outside, the tight end is coached to lock up with the defender (keep his hat on him) and run the safetyman deep. This gives the ball carrier the option of cutting off the tight end's block.

Against the rolling defensive secondary, where the cornerback is taught to roll up to the outside and contain the sweep, the tight end is coached to gain as much width as possible and go for the defender's outside knee. The blocker must fight to get his head outside of the cornerman's outside knee and keep his body between the cornerman and the sweeping ball carrier. Once the blocker has committed himself and has thrown at the outside knee of the defender, he is coached to roll his hips at contact and continue rolling after the defender. (Diagram 13-15.) The coaching point behind the blocker's rolling after the technique is that he may be able to trip up the defender's legs and force the secondary defender to concentrate on getting rid of the rolling blocker. This forces the cornerman to take his eyes off the carrier, to get rid of the blocker, just long enough for the pitchman to make a successful break. The primary purpose of the tight end's block is to chop down the cornerman, and the secondary feature of rolling is to tie up the defender's legs in case the blocker does not knock the defender down on the chop block. (Diagram 13-18.)

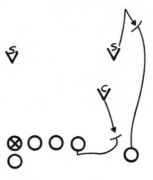

Diagram 13-18

CHAPTER FOURTEEN

Additional "I" Triple Option Plays

Fullback Dive Blocking Adjustments

Since the fullback may break outside of the frontside tackle's block, as well as inside, the offensive tight end is coached to chug the #3 defender if he is continually crashing down on the fullback play. The tight end may also be called upon to chug the #3 defender if he continually veers down and hits the quarterback after the hand off to the fullback. (Diagram 14-1.) Thus the quarterback is basically unprotected; the #3 defender has an open shot at the ball handler.

The chug technique by the tight end is also useful when the defensive #2 and #3 defenders have a cross charge, which drives the #3 defender down tight over the outside shoulder of the offensive tackle's original position, with the #2 defender looping to the #3 man's original position. (Diagram 14-2.) The chug technique on this defensive stunt would automatically open up the point of the attack on the fullback base play maneuver.

The fullback dive play also breaks inside of the offensive tackle's block. As long as this play is a consistent gainer, the defense must respect this dive play, which sets up the Triple Option "I" and the Double Option "I" plays. (Diagram 14-1.)

As soon as the defenders outside of the crease attempt to tackle the fullback from the outside-in angle, the quarterback's pitch or keep maneuver becomes a big play.

The Fullback "I" Dive play also forces the Oklahoma (52) playside defensive tackle to veer in to stop the fullback or step out to tackle the quarterback. This means the defensive tackle can no longer try to hang on the line of scrimmage and attempt to tackle either the fullback or quarterback. Thus, the Fullback Dive "I" takes away this tackle's lazy choice.

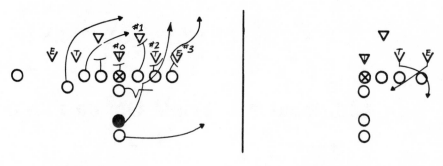

Diagram 14-1   **Diagram 14-2**

Many basic defenses today are equipped to take away the fullback dive off the Triple Option play. Therefore, we coach our quarterback to call the basic Fullback "I" Dive play to take advantage of these basic defenses.

Against the Eagle defense, the most advantageous blocking call would call for a double team block on the defenive tackle. If the double teamming offensive linemen could get inside 45 degree movement on the defensive tackle, the fullback could hug the double team block and break across the line of scrimmage. The chug technique by the tight end, along with his maximum split, could delay the #2 defender just long enough to break the fullback loose. (Diagram 14-3.)

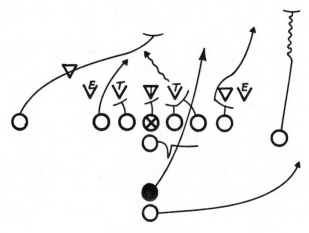

Diagram 14-3

The above technique is also true of the Wide 44 defensive align-ment. (Diagram 14-4.) The chug block by the tight end features a successful Fullback Base play.

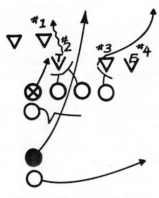

Diagram 14-4

Fullback Dive—"Wall-It"

The Fullback Dive play is run with one-on-one blocking to which we give a key call, "Wall-it." Wall-it means the interior linemen (both tackles, guards, and offensive center) block the interior defenders toward the initial Triple Option defensive pursuit in a literal wall-off fashion.

This means the quarterback steps back a little farther than usual and hands the ball off just as he normally does on the Triple Option play. As soon as the fullback gets the ball he cuts sharply to his left (Diagram 14-5), and breaks behind the wall-off blocking technique by

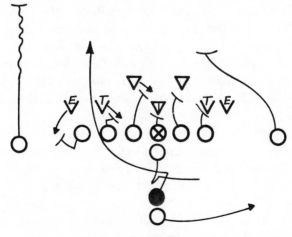

Diagram 14-5

the interior offensive linemen. The apparent Triple Option play increases the interior defenders' pursuit away from the offensive backs' initial steps. All of the blockers block the defenders the way they want to go and then wall off their secondary reaction moves before they can sufficiently recover to react to the sharp counter move by the diving fullback. As soon as the quarterback hands the ball off to the fullback, he continues down the line of scrimmage just like he was running his regular Triple Option course. The tailback also sprints away from the point of the attack, carrying out his Triple Option course. (Diagram 14-5.)

The defensive tight end, toward the point of the attack, is the only blocker who does not wall-off block to his right. The tight end merely sets up and blocks the containing defensive end's contain route. As soon as the defensive end steps to the outside, the tight end continues to block the defender to the outside. The blocking technique by the tight end is the same technique used by a pass defender in pass protection.

The Inside Fold Block—Fullback Dive

The inside fold block between the frontside offensive guard and tackle is often used against the Oklahoma defense. The inside fold block calls for the frontside (playside) guard to block on the defensive tackle (#2), and then the frontside offensive tackle takes a set step (allowing the frontside guard to pass) and folds to the inside to block the inside linebacker head on (#1). Normally the playside linebacker will begin to scrape toward the offensive tackle hole, so the folding offensive tackle has a good angle on the moving frontside defensive inside Oklahoma linebacker. The offensive center is coached to cut off the middle guard (#0), while the tight end chugs into the frontside defensive end and then continues downfield. The backside guard is coached to cut off the backside inside defensive linebacker's (#1) shuffling route. The backside offensive tackle must block the backside defensive #2 man and stay with this defender, because there are times when the fullback may decide to cut the Fullback Dive play all the way back behind the center's block on the middle guard. (Diagram 14-6.)

The inside fold block between the frontside offensive guard and tackle is also a fine call against the 44 defense. Since the frontside inside 44 linebacker is coached to scrape toward the off tackle hole, the folding tackle has an excellent blocking angle on this scrapping linebacker. If the frontside #1 defender scrapes himself beyond the defensive #2 man and into the off tackle hole, the offensive playside guard checks to the inside, for backside flow, and continues downfield and blocks the first odd jersey who shows. (Diagram 14-7.) The front-side tackle again blocks the outside #2 defender, while the tight end chugs the outside #3 defender and continues downfield. The offensive center is taught to check for a blitz by the frontside #1 linebacker and then block back on the backside #1 defensive linebacker. The backside guard and tackle block the defenders to their outside. The backside tackle then releases from his outside block and blocks out on the defensive outside linebacker (#4) to cut off his defensive pursuit.

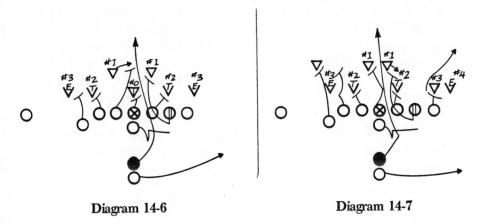

Diagram 14-6   Diagram 14-7

The Center Fold—Fullback Dive

The center Fold block is executed by the offensive center and the offensive guard to the point of the attack. The center first fires out into the defensive #1 man, and the frontside guard executes an inside fold block. The blocking frontside guard must delay long enough for the center to block out on his assigned man; then, the guard steps around to the inside, off the center's tail. This delay helps to set up the linebacking #0 defender. The fullback's apparent Triple Option path forces the middle linebacker to scallop toward the offensive crease. As soon as the fullback cuts inside, the frontside defender has been drawn out of position and the frontside guard has a fine angle block on the #0 defender. (Diagram 14-8.)

"I" Split End Reverse

A proven long gainer for the Triple Option attack has been the Split End Reverse play. This play which is run off the Triple Option minimizes the defensive team's pursuit and makes the quick rotating secondaries honest.

The split end sets and then drops back and begins to run his reverse course. The split end is assigned to catch the quarterback's soft, dead knuckle-like ball lateral.

The slot back is assigned to block the backside #3 defender, and he must stop the defender's penetration. The backside offensive tackle blocks backside #2, while the backside offensive guard is assigned to block the backside #1 defender, using his head-on block. The offensive center blocks #0, backside #1 area.

The frontside offensive blockers must first stop their respective defender's penetration and then begin to pull toward their second assignments at the point of the attack. The frontside guard blocks #1 and pulls along the line of scrimmage, and then peels back toward the outside just in front of the tight end's original position, looking for a pursuing defender to block. The frontside tackle blocks #2 and then pulls to the left toward the point of the attack and kicks out on the first defender who shows. The offensive tight end pulls to his left and makes an "O" or circle-like path so that the guard ends up just behind the tight end's original position. The guard peels back and looks back toward the inside to pick up the contain man or any defender who may be trailing the end around. (Diagram 14-9.)

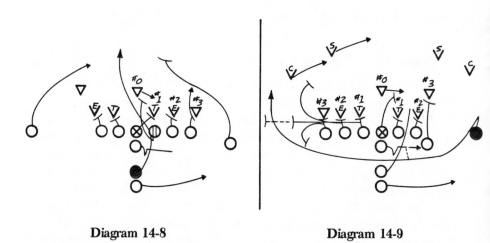

Diagram 14-8   Diagram 14-9

Diagram 14-10 illustrates how the Split End's Reverse is run against the Revert or Bubble defense.

Tailback Cross Buck

The tailback cross buck is a trap-like maneuver which takes advantage of defenses which like to penetrate deeply off the corners or against the quick pursuing defenses. The blocking rules for this cross buck play are as follows:

Flanker	—Run off deep outside one third defender.
Tight End	—Block the first defender to the inside.
Frontside Tackle	—Block #2.
Frontside Guard	—Block #1.
Center	—Block #0, Backside #1 area.
Backside Guard	—Pull and trap block first defender outside of tight end's block.
Backside Tackle	—Crossfield, block in front of point of the attack.
Split End	—Block deep one third area.

Diagram 14-11 illustrates how the above blocking rules apply to the Oklahoma defense.

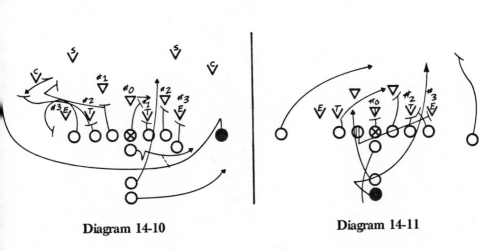

Diagram 14-10   **Diagram 14-11**

The backfield maneuver emphasizes a quick option ride to the fullback opposite the point of the attack and then steps directly backward and hands the ball off, with the left hand, to the tailback. The offensive drives over the area vacated by the pulling left guard, making a good fake into the line. A stutter step away from the point of the attack is executed by the tailback, and then he drives off his back foot toward the point of the attack. The left arm is lifted high, making a good pocket, and then the running back sets his course off the outside hip of the tight end. Since the pulling guard blocks out on the first defender to show outside of the tight end's block, the ball carrier cuts inside of this trap block.

Against the 44 defense, the pulling guard kicks out on the outside linebacker who lines up over the tight end. The offense does not block the defensive end, because this defender is responsible for containing the sweep and this defensive assignment takes him out of the play. The offensive frontside tackle and guard double team the defensive tackle, as the offensive guard makes the double team call, opening up the point of the attack. The tight end blocks down to the inside, looking for the frontside inside linebacker's pursuit course. The center selects the second phase of his blocking assignment and blocks the backside area (backside linebacker); but, first, the center checks for the possibility of the frontside linebacker's shooting the gap. Thus, his blocking course is a step to the frontside first, looking up the frontside inside linebacker and then blocking the backside area. (Diagram 14-12.)

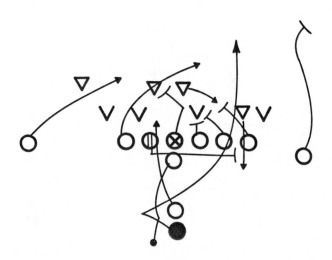

Diagram 14-12

From the 44 defense, many teams jump into a 7-Diamond-like alignment. If this happens, the offensive blockers merely follow their blocking rules. (With the center blocking #0 and the frontside guard blocking the #1 defender.) The #1 defender in the 7-Diamond defense is the middle linebacker, which gives the offensive guard a good blocking angle. A fine blocking angle is also set up when the offensive frontside tackle blocks the #2 defender to his inside. The tight end blocks down on the #3 man and the pulling backside guard traps out on the first defender outside of the tight end's block. (Diagram 14-13.)

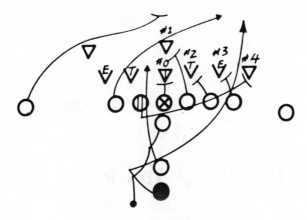

Diagram 14-13

CHAPTER FIFTEEN

"I" Passing Attack

Triple Option Carol Pass

The Triple Option pass begins with a quick fake to the fullback, and then the quarterback sprints out to the strong side of the formation. The flanker runs a curl pattern, while the tight end runs the arrow pattern—thus, the term Carol Pass.

This is one of the most difficult passes to stop because the defender, who is coached to cover the flat area, is influenced to come up out of his flat area to insure against the sprint out route by the sprinting quarterback. As soon as this defender moves up slightly, the tight end's angle arrow pattern is open. (Diagram 15-1.)

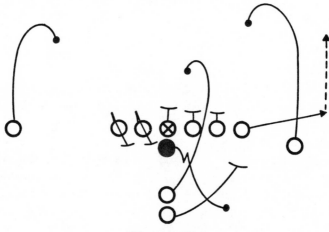

Diagram 15-1

When the flanker curls back toward the middle of the field, his pattern is actually going against the flow or revolving movement of the defensive secondary. The quarterback's fake and sprint action allows the flanker to run a deeper than normal curl (15 yards) and allows the receiver to set himself before the quarterback delivers the ball.

The tailback's frontside blocking route gives the quarterback three blockers to the sprint side of the offense. If the defense rushes only two defenders versus the pass, the tailback is then coached to run a circle or loop pass pattern. There is no use in holding a back in the pass protection scheme if there is no one to block. Releasing the third potential receiver into the strong side places all the more pressure on the strong side pass defenders. (Diagram 15-2.)

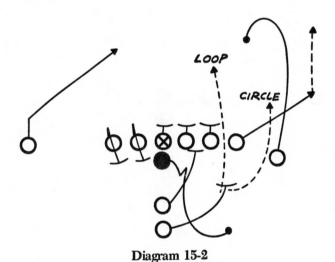

Diagram 15-2

Triple Roll Counter "I" Pass

The defensive draw off the Triple Roll Counter pass results from a good ride fake to the fullback, simulating a Triple Option right play. After riding the fullback to the strong side of the offense, the quarterback pulls the ball out of the fullback's stomach and begins a counter rolling action toward the split end's side. The quarterback has the option to continue running the ball on his bootleg run around the short side corner, or he can choose to pull up inside of the right guard's pulling action block and throw to the split end, running a deep post pattern or to the flanker back running his shallow drag pass pattern. (Diagram 15-3.)

The tight end and right tackle fire out and then reset to set up a wall to the bootlegging quarterback's blind side.

The right guard is coached to pull out and belly back off the line of scrimmage, so he can block the defender who rushes from the #3 defensive area.

The center blocks #0 or helps out wherever the line blocking needs help.

The frontside offensive left guard and left tackle fire out into their respective #1 and #2 defenders and then drop back to guard the line of scrimmage. Both of these frontside blockers must seal off any defensive seepage. (Diagram 15-3.)

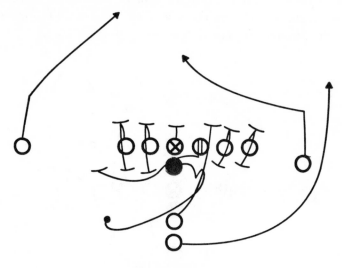

Diagram 15-3

Fullback Release Pass Versus The Oklahoma Defense

From the "I" alignment, the Fullback Release pass is an excellent route to take advantage of the inside strong side linebacker's drop to the tight end's hook zone. The fullback is coached to set up to block the strong side's inside linebacker vacated area. This is a delayed pass pattern by the fullback, and he does not run his inside releases until the linebacker has taken off in the tight end's direction. The fullback is coached to take the pass over his inside left shoulder. The receiver has a tendency to take off before he has the ball because he usually catches the ball with no one around him; therefore, the receiver must be cautioned to catch the ball, put it away, and then run with it.

The tailback also checks the weakside linebacker and blocks him if he blitzes. The tailback also may run a release route, if the weakside linebacker sprints to his outside area to defend against the split end's curl pass pattern. (Diagram 15-4.)

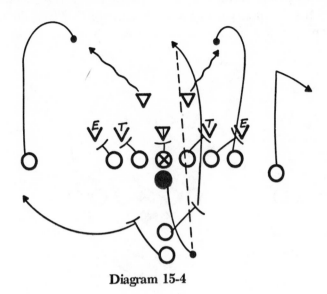

Diagram 15-4

"I" Sprint Right Flood Pass

A strong running-passing threat at quarterback helps to make the sprint out pass a bona fide offensive threat off the Pro "I" formation. The quarterback is coached to sprint out and turn upfield just prior to throwing his pass. A coaching point for the quarterback is to level his shoulders to the line of scrimmage just prior to throwing the pass. The sprint out quarterback must throw the ball off his front foot. (Diagram 15-5.)

The flood pass pattern moves three pass receivers into two defensive secondary zones. This forces one pass defender to cover the two receivers within his assigned zone. The three potential flood receivers are in excellent peel blocking position whenever the quarterback decides to keep the ball and run.

The line blocking protection is a reach blocking technique by both guards, center, and the frontside tackle. The backside tackle begins to reach and then retreats to pick off or wall off any trailing defender.

The fullback sneaks out of the backfield by executing a fake sprint out pass protection block on the first defender outside of the frontside offensive tackle's block; then, the fullback angles out into the flat. The tailback then picks up the first defender outside of the frontside tackle's reach block.

The "I" Sprint Flood Pass is an excellent pass against a man to man pass defense. This is especially true versus the goal line defense, where the secondary is in a man to man defense. Usually the fullback is open for a touchdown pass just a yard inside the goal line.

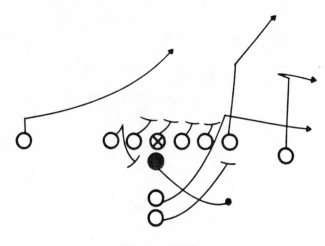

Diagram 15-5

Drop Back Pass Protection From the Pro "I"

Although the "I" set is a most advantageous sprint out pass formation, it can also be used as a successful drop back pass defense. Basically the center blocks over, strong side. The guard's rules are: Block the first lineman from the center. The tackle's rules are: Block the second lineman away from the center. The set backs check the inside linebacker first and the outside linebacker second. If no linebacker blitzes, the back is coached to get into the pass pattern by

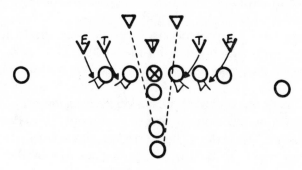

Diagram 15-6

finding an open area in the opposition's pass defense. Diagrams 15-6 and 15-7 illustrate the above blocking rules.

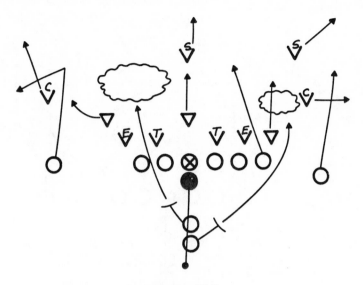

Diagram 15-7

Coaching Point: See the drop back pass protection rules utilizing the Veer or Split Pro pass attack in Chapter 19.

Drop Back Pass Versus The Two Deep Zone Secondary

Since the two deep pass defense is responsible for the deep one half secondary zones, we like to throw to our receivers just beyond the underneath five pass defenders. In Diagram 15-8, the split end releases off the line of scrimmage to his outside and runs an up pass pattern close to the sidelines. The passer times his receiver so the ball will arrive into the receiver's hands at about 16 to 18 yards deep. This means the ball will reach the receiver in the gray area between the underneath coverage and the deep left safetyman covering his deep one half zone.

Since the two deep safetymen line up on their respective hash marks and drop straight backwards on the marks, we also like to stretch the two deep safetymen as wide as possible and then hit the pass to the vacated inside area. Diagram 15-9 illustrates the drop back passer throwing to the inside receiver (tight end) on a semi-delayed inside route. The deep right safetyman must drop back to his outside to defend against the quick outside up pass pattern by the wide flanker back. The passer can look the deep safety defender to the outside (set his body and look to the outside receiver) and hit the tight end just as he cuts to the inside. Therefore, the inside post pattern (Diagram 15-9), or an inside curl pass splits the two wide zoning safety pass defenders in half.

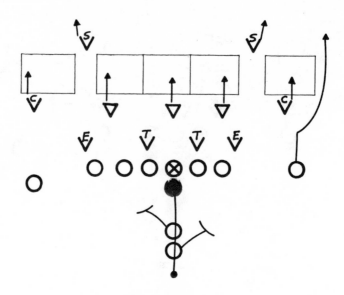

Diagram 15-8

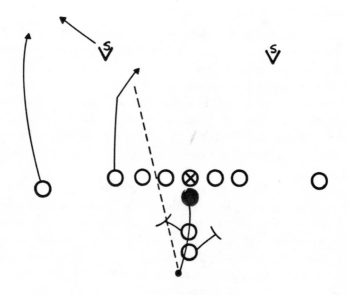

Diagram 15-9

The antithesis of the previous pass play is also used, whereby the tight end holds the right safetyman to the inside of the hash mark, while the flanker runs an inside-up-flag route. The passer releases the ball so the flanker receives the ball just as he takes his first or second step to the outside for his final flag cut. (Diagram 15-10.)

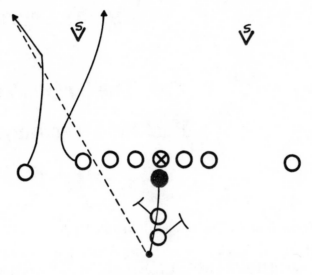

Diagram 15-10

CHAPTER SIXTEEN

The Triple Veer
Backfield Techniques

Veer Triple Option's Quarterback-Diveback Mesh

The quarterback takes a short six inch lead step on a 30 degree angle toward the dive back. His eyes are focused upon his first defensive key (first defender to show outside of the playside offensive tackle). The second step is with the (left) backside foot. The quarterback is taught to step down the line of scrimmage and not back on the 45 degree angle, as described in the Wishbone and I rides. (Diagram 16-1.) The next step with the right foot hits an imaginary point about

Diagram 16-1

one and one half yards behind, and a foot outside of, the offensive guard's original inside foot position. As this foot hits the ground, the ball handler is coached to extend the ball toward the diveback's pocket. The quarterback is coached to push or poke the ball into the fullback's pocket. There is no ride to the diving back. As the ball is

178

extended to the diving back, the far foot is brought parallel to the lead or reach step in a dragging action. As the quarterback pokes the ball into the dive back's pocket, the ball handler's shoulders should be parallel to the sidelines. The drag step should be a soft adjustment step, and the quarterback should not shift his weight to the drag foot. (Diagram 16-2.) Actually the quarterback steps with the near foot and then makes a hop step with the backside foot (Drag Step).

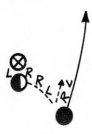

Diagram 16-2

The quarterback is taught to set his course close to and parallel to the line of scrimmage. Since the dive back is lined up on the outside foot of the guard, his dive route is actually run away from the quarterback's path. Therefore, the quarterback extends the ball to the dive back, while keeping his eyes on the dive key (first defensive key). The ball handler must be careful to push the ball toward the dive back rather than ride the ball into the line of scrimmage. (Diagram 16-3.) To a large extent, the responsibility of the quarterback-dive back mesh lies with the dive back. It is the dive back's assignment to place his nose directly into the center of the extended football to insure the perfect mesh, since the quarterback is taught to focus his eyes on the dive key.

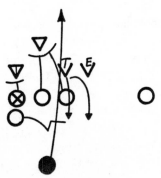

Diagram 16-3

The quarterback must feel his pocket step when approaching the quarterback-dive man mesh, because the ball handler's eyes are glued on the dive option key. The more the quarterback practices his steps, the more smoothly the quarterback is able to execute his approach steps. The field general should not try to rush his steps on the approach to the mesh area. The correct execution of the read, ball extension, and steps are more important than the quarterback's speed.

The ball handler is coached to keep his elbows close to his body and maintain a two hand grip on the ball at all times. He should point the ball directly at the first key.

The difference between the Veer hand off and the Wishbone and "I" mesh is that, in the Veer, the dive man is responsible for the correct mesh. The fullback sets his nose for the middle of the extended football, as the quarterback moves more down the line of scrimmage rather than reaching back and giving the fullback a ride fake as in the Wishbone and "I" sets. There is no ride in the Veer hand off, as the quarterback is coached to thrust the ball into the dive back's pocket.

Quarterback-Diveman Mesh

The quarterback must place the ball into the diveman's pocket at the same spot on all Triple Option plays. Since the quarterback must read the first defensive key, the perfection of the mesh between these two backs is paramount in the overall timing of the Triple Option series.

The dive man must set up the mesh by lining up his nose on the center of the ball, held in the quarterback's extended hands. The diveman's responsibility of perfecting the mesh is by the fact that the quarterback must glue his eyes on the first (dive) key.

Veer Hand Off

The dive back is coached to make his pocket similar to the pocket described by the fullback in Chapter 4. The inside elbow must be up, so the quarterback is able to slide the ball in or pull the ball out of the dive man's pocket at the last moment. The dive back must center the football with his nose since the quarterback moves down the line, pointing the ball at the dive key. As the ball is placed into the dive back's pocket, the dive man's lower arm accepts the ball. He must not clamp down upon the ball or try to grab the ball away from the ball handler. It is the quarterback's option alone, whether to hand the ball off or to pull the ball out of the pocket. On the hand off, the quarterback must feel the ball securely in the dive back's pocket before he hands the ball off. The ball handler's far hand is the last hand that leaves the ball. The near hand and back of the quarterback's near wrist is used to feel the ball into the diving back's pocket. Once the ball is handed off, the quarterback is encouraged to continue down the line a couple of steps to practice his second level read on the pitch-keep key.

The hand off dive play hits so quickly that the dive back is on top of the safetyman often before the deep back is in his break down defensive tackling position.

Collision Area

More time must be spent with the quarterback stepping around the collision area in the Veer formation than when the fullback is lined up directly behind the center and is designated as the dive back. The reason behind this coaching point is that the Veer optioning quarterback is sprinting more down the line of scrimmage, and his path has a greater chance of being jammed, than reaching back and riding the fullback in the Wishbone and the "I" Triple Options.

After the quarterback fakes to the dive back, he must be ready to step around any penetration by the defense. Then, he must step back on his course as soon as possible, so he will maintain the correct four by four yard ratio with the trailing back in the event the ball handler decides to pitch the ball.

The quarterback focuses his eyes on the dive key as soon as he receives the ball from the center. As he extends the ball to the dive back, the ball handler must make the decision whether to give the ball off to the dive back or keep the ball and read the second level key.

If the defender is responsible for the dive (first defensive key) steps upfield or steps to his outside, the quarterback is coached to give the ball to the dive back. (Diagram 16-3.)

Should the dive key close or step to the inside to tackle the dive back, the ball handler is taught to keep the ball. This means the quarterback must pull the ball out of the dive back's pocket and read the second pitch or keep key. (Diagram 16-4.)

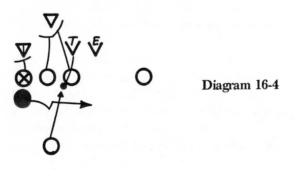

Diagram 16-4

Teaching The Pitch-Keep (Reading the Second Key)

After pulling the ball out of the dive man's pocket, the quarterback is coached to sprint parallel one and one half yards down the line of scrimmage to challenge the pitch-keep key (second key). The quarterback must be ready to deviate from a strict parallel course down the line of scrimmage, because he may have to step around the first key collision area if the defender penetrates and tackles the dive man behind the line of scrimmage. If the collision takes place, the ball handler is coached to merely step around this congested area and then regain his parallel challenge course. (Diagram 16-5.) The quarterback must be made to realize his speed will allow him to outrun most four point or squatting defensive tackles. (Diagram 16-6.)

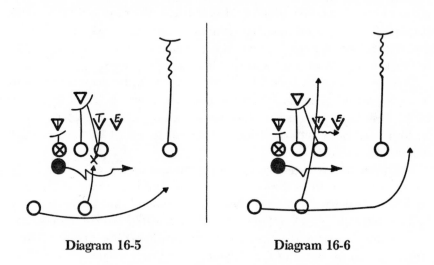

Diagram 16-5   Diagram 16-6

The quarterback must be ready to make his pitch to the trailing back or his keeper play while running at full speed. The ball handler is responsible to make the pitch, if the second key closes down the line to attack the quarterback or merely freezes (squats) in his normal defensive end position. (Diagram 16-7.)

If the second key steps straight upfield or feathers to the outside (widens), the quarterback is coached to keep the ball, driving off his back foot, and turn directly upfield. (Diagram 16-8.)

The quarterback keeper play is usually most successful from the Triple Veer Series (split backs), because the quarterback is working more closely to the line of scrimmage than he does using the Wishbone or "I" backfield formations. The Veer keeper also hits quicker, because the quarterback does not have to reach back on a 45 degree angle and attack the second key off the line of scrimmage, as in the Wishbone or "I" formation.

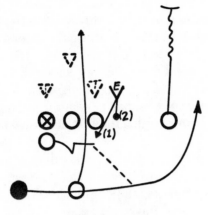

Diagram 16-7

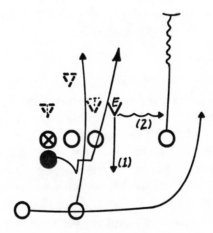

Diagram 16-8

Teaching the Quarterback How To Make the Pitch

The quarterback must be able to make the pitch sprinting down the line of scrimmage at full speed. The pitch should be made with one hand. The pitch is made with the right hand while sprinting to the right, and with the left hand when sprinting to the left. The quarterback should point the same foot as the pitching hand directly at the area or target to which he is aiming the pitch out. On all Triple

Option plays, the quarterback is coached to thick "pitch," first, and run the ball on the keeper only when the second defensive key definitely takes away the pitch out, by stringing or feathering wide or stepping straight across the line of scrimmage.

When running the Triple Option play toward the split end, the quarterback must be taught to be ready to pitch the ball immediately after the quarterback-dive mesh, because the defender usually attacks the quarterback right now to the short side. If the quarterback is unable to read the second defensive key correctly, he should continue down the line of scrimmage and challenge the defender as soon as possible. This forces the defender to commit himself quickly, so the ball handler has a clearer read of the first defensive key outside of the dive key.

The pitch should be a push knuckle-ball type to make it easy for the backside running back to handle. The quarterback should never try to breakdown or squat down just prior to the pitch out. Once the pitch out has been made, the quarterback must follow through with the pitch arm and follow the flight of the ball with the quarterback's eyes right into the pitchman's hands. The ball should be pitched above the pitchman's waist, with the proper lead, so the trailing running back does not have to break stride to take the pitch out and continue on his wide outside course.

Teaching The Keeper

The quarterback keeps the ball only when the second defensive key (outside key) takes away the pitch out play. The quarterback can help open up the keeper hole by actually faking the pitch out, extending both arms and showing the ball in a fake pitch action, and faking the second key to the outside and then keeping the ball and turning up inside of the off tackle hole. The keeper play is most successful when the quarterback makes his turn up to the inside, while he is sprinting down the line of scrimmage at full speed.

An important coaching point for the quarterback, who continually looses his footing when turning upfield, is to emphasize cutting off the back foot. If the quarterback attempts to cut off the front foot, he will lose his footing repeatedly, especially in damp weather.

If the quarterback is unable to get a quick read on the outside (second) key, he is coached to challenge the outside key. If the defensive end continues to widen or holds his position on the line of scrimmage, the ball handler is coached to play it safe and keep the ball, cutting into the off tackle hole.

The success of the keeper play is insured by the holding fake on the inside defender's pursuit by the quarterback-dive back's fake. At least one outside defender must be assigned to stop the outside pitch out. If the one defender who has been assigned to tackle the quarterback misses his assignment, either mentally or by missing the tackle on the quarterback, the ball handler has an excellent chance for success.

As soon as the quarterback turns up inside on the keeper, he is coached to hold the ball in the outside hand, while the inside hand covers the ball, minimizing any chance for a fumble by the quarterback.

Dive Back

The dive back lines up four yards away from the tip of the football and splits the outside foot of the offensive guard with the dive back's midline.

The dive back is coached to take a short six inch step with the outside foot, aiming for a target area between the playside guard and tackle. The second step is with the backside foot; and on the third step with the outside foot, the dive back accepts the hand off or the fake. Regardless whether the dive back receives the ball or not, he is coached to break to the outside off the playside offensive tackle's block. Running the normal Triple Option play, the dive back should never run inside of the playside offensive tackle's block. (Diagram 16-9.)

When accepting the ball from the quarterback, the dive back is taught to lift the inside elbow high and rotate the thumb of this hand slightly away from his body. This thumb rotation raises the elbow higher and cuts down upon the chances of the hand off striking the elbow during the quarterback-dive back mesh. The small finger of the outside hand should be placed on the dive man's belt buckle. The elbow of the bottom hand should be the shield against the quarterback pushing the ball too far through the pocket. If the quarterback does not give the ball to the dive back, he must be a fake first and a blocker second. An alert blocker can cut off a key inside pursuing defender helping the pitch out or the keeper play to break away for a substantial gainer. If no defender shows from the inside, the faker should continue his route downfield and block the first odd-colored jersey he finds. The dive back must continue faking downfield, holding his left elbow in high right hand and vice versa. Both arms should swing slightly, emulating the dive back's two hand ball carrying technique.

The dive back must be cautioned to use a soft fold with the bottom hand when accepting the ball. The dive man must not clamp down upon the ball as soon as he sees daylight. The responsibility for the hand off or the pull out is the quarterback's, and his alone.

Since the dive back on the veer is running a wider angle away from the hand off than the Wishbone or "I" fullback (lined up directly behind the center), the dive back must run directly for the football. The dive back places his nose toward the middle of the extended football thus helping the quarterback-dive back's mesh, since the quarterback's eyes are fastened on the first (dive) key.

As soon as the dive back enters the crease (seam), opened by the offensive frontside linemen between the original position and the playside guard and tackle, he must have his shoulders squared off (parallel) to the line of scrimmage. The dive back's path must be constant to both sides of the center, so that the mesh will be consistently smooth.

If the dive back focuses his eyes on the first defender to show outside of the offensive playside tackle's block, he will usually be able to anticipate whether the quarterback will give the dive back the ball or pull the football out of the dive back's pocket.

Once the dive back gets the football, he must be running forward (shoulders parallel to the line of scrimmage) at full speed. The ball carrier must have the proper body lean so as to break through any arm or off balanced side tackle at the line of scrimmage. We tell our dive back to bust up there just like a fullback does when he is a couple of yards away from the opponent's goal line. The dive man must think he is going to get the ball on every play so he will always be going at full steam. (Diagram 16-9.)

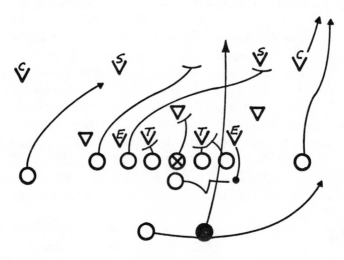

Diagram 16-9

Pitchman

The pitchman's alignment is to split the backside offensive guard's outside foot with the back's midline. The back should be lined up four yards from the ball. The balanced parallel stance should be employed so the offensive back is able to take off in any direction.

The pitchman is taught to take a short open step parallel to the line of scrimmage. He is coached to take a course which will sprint him directly through the dive back's original position. This parallel path should place the pitchman in a perfect position to receive the pitch out from the quarterback. This position is four yards outside and four yards deeper than the ball handler.

Running the Triple Option to the split end's side, the pitchman must be ready to receive the pitch quickly, because the defender who is responsible for attacking the quarterback is closer to the quarterback to the split end's side than he is to the tight end's side. The pitchman is coached to run his course just as if he were running a 100 yard dash. The pitchman does not belly his course until after he receives the pitch out. The pitchman's assignment is to sprint for width to put pressure on the defender who has been assigned to contain the pitch out. Once the quarterback decides to turn downfield on the keeper, the pitchman must continue to maintain his four-four yard ration to the ball carrier to be ready for a possible lateral. The wide blockers are coached to wall off the deep defenders; thus, the ball carrier is coached to run for width to get outside of the blocking wall.

The ball carrier is taught to hold the ball in the outside arm to keep the ball away from the defenders, and to afford the ball carrier

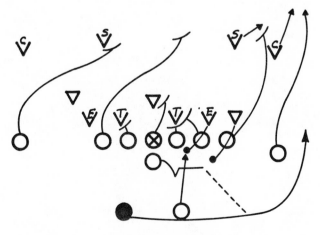

Diagram 16-10

the chance to use the inside arm to ward off the potential tacklers. The pitchman turns downfield when the offensive blocker is forced to block the stringing or feathering containing defender to the outside. (Diagram 16-10.)

Tight End's Kick Out Block

If the defensive contain man gains four to five yards penetration past the line of scrimmage, the tight end is coached to kick or block out this containing defender. The ball carrier is then taught to cut up inside of this inside-out block and then run for daylight. (Diagram 16-11.)

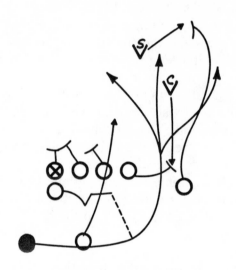

Diagram 16-11

CHAPTER SEVENTEEN

The Veer Triple Option

Quarterback's Parallel Triple Veer Path

The quarterback is coached to continue his parallel path down the line of scrimmage. If the ball handler does not hand the ball off to the dive back, he is instructed to continue along his course, parallel to the line of scrimmage, and challenge the second key. The only time the quarterback must step off his parallel path is when some defender penetrates across the line of scrimmage and tackles the dive man on the offensive side of the line of scrimmage. The quarterback is instructed to step around this collision and work to get back on course to challenge the next phase of his Triple Option assignment.

The quarterback is able to stay closer to the line of scrimmage on the Triple Veer, because he steps more parallel to fake to the veering running back, rather than backward to ride the fullback fake off the Triple I or Wishbone Triple Option attack.

Veer Punch Fake on the Triple Veer

Running the Veer Triple Option, the quarterback is taught not to ride the ball to the diving back; rather, the quarterback is coached to simply punch the ball at the dive back. The dive back's dive fake is the holding influence on the defense rather than a ride. Since the dive man is running away from the hand off area, the quarterback must be careful to punch the ball all the way into the dive back's far hip when he gives the dive man the ball.

The quarterback must keep two hands on the ball and think, "pitch," all the way, so that the dive back does not knock the ball out of the optioning ball handler's hands. The quarterback is coached to think, "pitch," as soon as he starts down the line of scrimmage.

Veer Pitch

The veer pitch should be made with a one hand (outside hand) lob. The pitch should be pushed to the tailing back and should resemble a jump shot in basketball. The quarterback should make the pitch when there is a four-four yard ratio between the quarterback and the pitchman. This means the pitchman should be four yards deeper than the quarterback and four yards outside of the quarterback. If these two backs get any closer, a defender may be able to play both offensive backs and may get a hand on the pitch.

The quarterback is coached to never force the pitch out. If there is any question whether the defender may get his hands on the pitch or the trailing back is not in a perfect receiving position, the quarterback is instructed to keep the ball.

The Veering Dive Fakes

Since both the running backs are called upon to dive into the crease, both veering offensive backs must be excellent fakers. We stress to all of our running backs that not all runners can be All American runners, but that all fakers can be All American fakers. All our backs are schooled in the theory that one good fake is worth more to our offense than one good block; because, a good fake not only sets up several blocks, but it may also pull other defenders off their respective pursuit courses. Minimizing the defensive pursuit often results in an offensive long gainer.

Blocking The 44 Blitz with the Triple Veer

When a particular opponent attempts to use the middle 44 blitz on a specific down, the veer offense blocks this technique as illustrated in Diagram 17-1.

The offensive center blocks the blitzing frontside linebacker to stop his penetration, while the frontside guard blocks the defensive tackle to the point of the attack. The right offensive tackle drives inside and the dive back cuts just outside the hip of the screening frontside offensive tackle. Both the left guard and left offensive tackle cut off the defenders to the blockers' inside. The left backside offensive guard must use a quick flat cut off blocking technique to stop the defensive penetration of the backside #1 defender.

Triple Veer Option Versus The Revert Defense

The Revert defense is one half of a bubble with the split side tackle lining up on the offensive guard's outside shoulder (23), the split side linebacker lining up over the offensive tackle (44), and the defensive split side end lining up on the line of scrimmage one yard outside of the offensive tackle (6). (Diagram 17-2.)

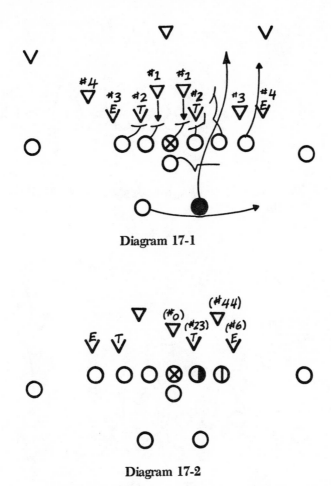

Diagram 17-1

Diagram 17-2

If the short side linebacker is overly scrapping or pursuing to help on the threat of the pitch off the Triple Option, the quarterback should be informed by his blocking short side linemen or coaches in the press box of this technique. The quarterback should then give the ball to the dive man, and he will often run right by the scrapping reverted defensive linebacker. (Diagram 17-3.)

The Veer Option can also be run featuring a definite keeper by the quarterback or a pitch out to the trailing back. This means that the fullback is predetermined not to get the ball in the huddle. Thus, the fullback is assigned a definite blocking assignment. The fullback is coached to seal the middle linebacker off when attacking a Revert defense. (Diagram 17-4.) Now the split side offensive guard and tackle

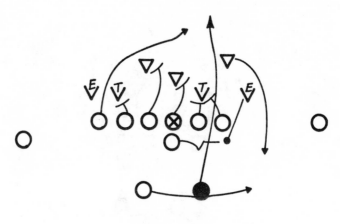

Diagram 17-3

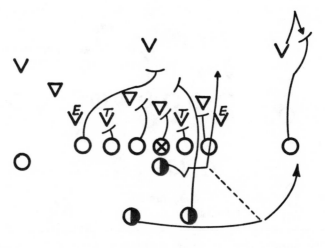

Diagram 17-4

block the defenders over them. The quarterback now attacks the defensive end and has the option of keeping or pitching off this defender. Both the keeper or the pitch has an excellent chance for success because of the seal off block on the inside linebacker by the dive man. (Diagram 17-4.)

The Triple Veer Versus the 65 Goal Line Defense

Defending against the Triple Veer attack, most 65 Goal Line defenses assign the middle linebacker to be responsible for the third receiver to the offensive strong side. Usually this middle linebacker is coached to line up on this potential receiver. (Diagram 17-5.) To run the Triple Veer against this goal line defense, we like to give the ball to the dive back since the defensive left tackle is often given the assignment of tackling the quarterback, while the defensive end must be responsible for the pitchman. (Diagram 17-5.)

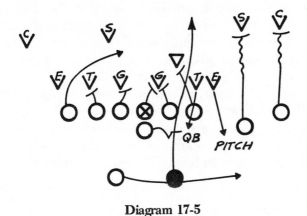

Diagram 17-5

Thus, the center and the right guard block the defensive guard, while the right offensive tackle blocks the linebacker. The dive man is given the ball and makes an option cut off the right tackle's discriminate block. The reason we use the term "discriminate block" is that we simply assign the offensive tackle the linebacker. The discrimination phase of the blocking allows the offensive blocker to take the defender any way the defender wants to go. If he just hangs there, we teach the blocker to drive the linebacker straight backwards. The ball carrier then takes his option and runs inside or outside of the offensive tackle's block.

Reverse Stance

The wide receiver on the right side uses a three point stance with the right hand down and the right foot slightly back. The weight should be placed on the up hand and up foot. The wide receiver's head should be slightly turned toward the quarterback, just enough to see the movement of the ball in case he is unable to hear the snap count. On Triple Option calls the wide receiver strives for an outside release to set up his stalk or slow block technique. The outside release enables the wide man his outside angle on the defender who will be assigned to cover the deep outside one third secondary area.

Inside Pass Release

Whenever a defender plays on the potential receiver's outside shoulder and forces the wide man to the inside, an inside release technique must be taught. The inside release's first step must be with the outside foot to stabilize the expected outside defensive blow. If the defender attempts to spear the potential receiver, driving the helmet across the wide lineman's body, the offensive player is coached to take a short inside step with the outside foot, while bringing up the outside forearm under the defender's neck. The outside arm under swing should follow through until the defender's head is removed from across the receiver's body.

A four point all out scramble release may be used also to release to the inside. It is almost impossible to knock a releasing player off balance when the potential receiver uses a four point scramble release. The inside release should be continually practiced because many defenders attempt to funnel all potential pass receivers to the inside.

Outside Pass Release

If the defender is head up and close to the potential pass receiver, the offensive man is taught to fake to the inside with a head and shoulder fake and then release to the outside. The first step to the outside should be a short quick step with the outside foot.

If the defender is on the outside shoulder, a slam release is another release used. The potential receiver drives his head straight into the numbers of the defender, just as if he were going to drive block the defender. The defender's first reaction is to get rid of the possible blocker. Once released, the potential receiver releases to the outside and gets into his pass pattern.

The scramble release (as described in the Inside Pass Release explanation) may also be used for an outside release.

CHAPTER EIGHTEEN

Veer Running Attack

The Double Option Off The Veer

The double option quarterback keep or pitch versus the normal second defense key is an excellent option to keep the defense honest against the Triple Option. Using split backs, it also gives the offensive backfield set a lead halfback to escort the pitchman around the corner. The double option is also a sound option play that makes the quarterback's option read easier than the Triple Option, because the ball handler only has to option off one defender. It also gives the quarterback more time to make up his mind whether to pitch or keep, because the normal first option (versus the Triple Option) is blocked by the offensive tackle to the point of the attack.

As soon as the quarterback receives the ball from the center, he puts the ball into his third hand (stomach) and takes a short lead step with his playside (frontside) foot. The second step is a cross over step, and then the quarterback moves down the line with his shoulders parallel to the line of scrimmage. The quarterback is taught to keep his eyes focused on the man he is to option, the third defender outside of the center. (Diagram 18-1.)

The lead back takes off in a course parallel to the line of scrimmage, just as the lead back is coached in the Wishbone lead back Triple Option coaching technique. The lead back is coached to block the contain man (the defensive safetyman on his invert course in Diagram 18-1). The right halfback is coached to execute a chop block on the defensive contain man, so the pitchman is able to turn the corner successfully. The ball carrier is taught to ride the outside hip of the lead back and to sweep wide unless the defensive cornerman forces the ball carrier to turn the play up inside of the contain assignment.

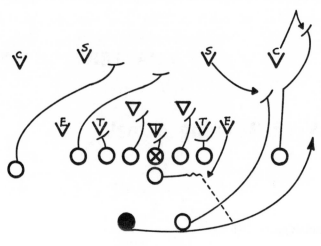

Diagram 18-1

The split end is directed to run off the defenders, who is responsible for the deep outside one third area, and to block him using an offensive outside-in angle block. The offensive tackle to the side of the attack is coached to use a scrambling reach block on the defensive tackle. Once the blocker gets his head, shoulders, and arms in front of his own defender, he is taught to continue to scramble the blocker so the tackle is unable to pursue the ball carrier. The offensive right guard blocks the offensive linebacker over him. This guard's block on the double option is a more difficult block than using the Triple Option, because there is no dive back to hold the frontside inside Oklahoma linebacker. Therefore, the offensive guard, to the side of the point of the attack, must quickly fire out on an angle to scramble the outside leg of the linebacker. Once the blocker has his head in front of the defender, he must keep scrambling on the defender, turning the blocker's butt in progression of the ball carrier. The center and backside offensive guard must cut off their assignments, while the backside tackle is instructed to chug the defensive tackle and then take a shallow crossfield course to make a block on one of the pursuing defenders. The backside defensive end cuts off the man to his outside and follows the backside offensive tackle on a shallow crossfield course.

Against the 44 defense, the blocking assignments are illustrated in Diagram 18-2. The split end uses a crack block and picks off the playside offensive linebacker. The right offensive tackle demonstrates a combo block where he drives in on the defensive tackle then chugs off to pick up the frontside inside 44 linebacker. The offensive right tackle does not perform the second part of his combo block until he is sure that the offensive right guard can handle the defensive tackle by himself. The center uses a reach block and cuts off the inside split linebacker. The backside inside linebacker is blocked by the backside offensive tackle. The backside offensive guard and tackle exchange their blocking assignments so that both of these blockers execute an inside fold block. The left guard has a good inside-out angle on the right defensive tackle, while the backside offensive tackle uses a scoop-like action to block the backside inside linebacker. The backside offensive tight end takes a shallow crossfield course, so that he is able to help out with a downfield block near the point of the attack. The flanker back simply blocks the deep backside safetyman in a two deep secondary or the backside one third zone versus a three deep secondary alignment.

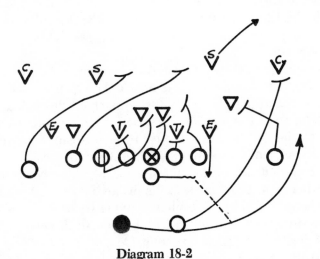

Diagram 18-2

Veer Counter Option

The Veer Counter Option toward the tight end is blocked similar to the counter option off the Wishbone formation. Against the Oklahoma defense, the offense blocks both the frontside linebacker and tackle to the side of the option. The tight end is then assigned to release outside of the #3 defender and blocks downfield. (Diagram 18-3.)

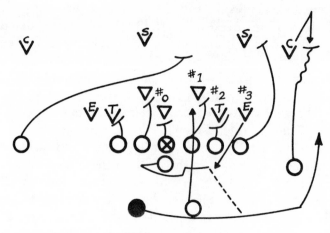

Diagram 18-3

The flanker runs off the defensive back, who is assigned to cover the deep outside one third area, or the cornerman who is assigned to play the flanker man to man. The center blocks the middle guard, while the backside guard and tackle block the defender on their outside shoulders. The split end is taught to block the deep middle one third zone.

The quarterback is instructed to take one step in the opposite direction of the ultimate point of attack. The quarterback steps with the left foot, and then he is coached to push off this foot and reverse his body to go in the opposite direction. The frontside running back dives into the gap between the center-guard gap. The quarterback makes a quick ball fake to the dive man, then focuses his eyes on the first defender outside of the offensive tackle. If the tackle attacks the ball handler as in Diagram 18-3, he makes a one hand pitch with his outside hand (right) to the trailing running back.

The dive back is coached to set a course directly between the original position between the frontside guard-center gap. He first takes a stutter step with his left foot to the left and then dives straight ahead.

The trailing back also makes a stutter step to his left and then sweeps toward the right end on a course parallel to the lines of scrimmage. The left halfback is coached to watch the #3 defender and looks for the quarterback to pitch, if this defender attacks the ball handler. The ball carrier stays to the outside, because both the tight end and flanker try to block the deep back to the inside so the ball carrier is able to turn the corner and stay to the outside for a long gainer.

Running the Veer Counter Option toward the split end's side is illustrated in Diagram 18-4. Again, the quarterback options off the #3 defender (linebacker) and pitches the ball if the #3 man attacks the ball handler. If the #3 man attempts to contain the potential pitch out, the ball handler is coached to keep the ball. Thus, the quarterback is coached to challenge the #3, defender, by running into his face, along his parallel course. The quarterback is coached to get the pitch off and to keep the ball only when the defender takes away the pitch play.

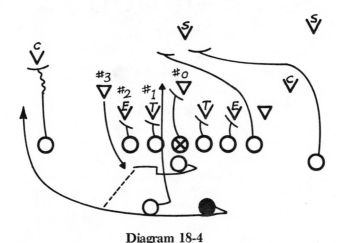

Diagram 18-4

If the #3 linebacker hangs on the line of scrimmage, we use a particular blocking adjustment where the split or short side offensive tackle is taught to pull around to the outside of his usual #2 blocking assignment and blocks the linebacker (#3). This means the quarterback now options off the penetrating defensive end (#2). This is an easier read for the quarterback, and, if the quarterback gets off a successful pitch, the ball carrier is able to turn the corner escorted by two offensive blockers (split end and split tackle). (Diagram 18-5.)

When the defense uses a rover defender to the offensive strong side, the Veer Counter Option play can still be a consistent gainer. Now the tight end is assigned to block the rover or monster back, while the flanker continues to run off the defender covering the deep outside one third area. (Diagram 18-6.)

If the defensive #3 man attacks the quarterback, the pitch is executed. The tight end is taught to step around the #3 defender and attempt to hook block the rover back to cut off the defender's outside contain course. The ball handler is coached to make a one hand push-pitch to the trailing running back, who should have a four-four yard ratio from the quarterback.

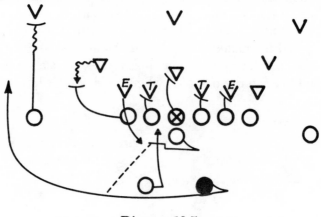

Diagram 18-5

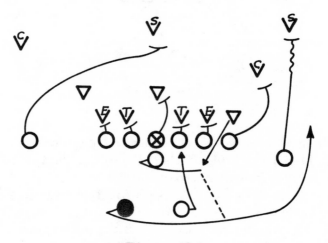

Diagram 18-6

CHAPTER NINETEEN

Veer's Drop Back Passes

Veer's Pass Protection

All of the pass protectors set up quickly and show pass right now, on all drop back pass plays. The blockers are taught to set up quickly for the charging defender. The pass blocker is coached to set up as soon as possible and give the rushing defender only one way to go. This means in our basic pocket pass protection, the blocker takes an inside-out blocking set up. He is taught to station himself between the rusher and the passer. The only route we want to give to the defender is the outside path. We take away the inside path because this is the shortest distance between the rusher and the passer.

The Split Pro Or Veer Formation Attack

The split or Veer formation is the finest drop back passing formation in the game today. With two quick wide pass receivers and split backs to either side, a natural drop back pocket is set up for the quarterback's straight drop back passing attack and the two wide receivers spread the defense. The two running backs are in excellent position to flare, circle, or loop out of their split back alignment. These two running backs are also in excellent blocking position to pick up the blitzing linebacker or screen the outside defensive ends around and in back of the pocket passer. (Diagram 19-1.)

This backfield set also gives the offense the continual threat of the quick pitch to either running back. The threat of the pro sweep to either side of the formation, along with the Veer Triple Option, gives this formation an explosive running attack to either the split or tight

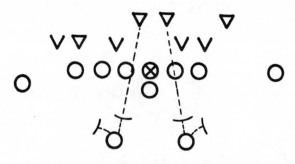

Diagram 19-1

end side of the line. The dive threat, along with the split backs' quick hitters, gives this formation a balanced running and passing attack.

The Veer Straight Drop Back Pass Protection

Since the split backfield or veer formation is an excellent drop back passing formation, we keep the drop back pass protection rules as simple as possible. These rules are as follows:

Center   —Over, strong side.
Guards   —First lineman from the center
Tackles   —Second lineman from the center
Backs   —Check inside linebackers first,
            outside linebackers second. If no
            linebackers blitz, get into the
            pass pattern. (Diagrams 19-2 and
            19-3.)

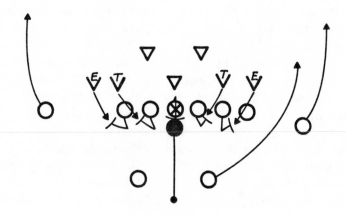

Diagram 19-2

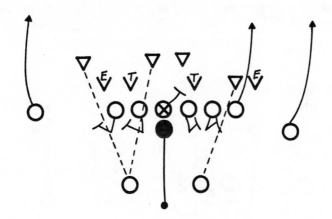

Diagram 19-3

If all eight defenders suddenly decided to attack the drop back pass off the 44 defense, all of the strong side defenders would be blocked and only the backside outside linebacker would be free to rush the passer. Since the backside outside rusher is a longer distance away from the passer than the weak or short side linebacker, the passer should be able to get off a quick successful flair control pass. (Diagram 19-4.)

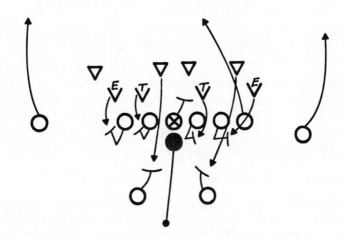

Diagram 19-4

If the quarterback expects an eight man rush, he simply calls maximum pass protection, and the tight end remains in the pass protection and both sets backs block to the split or weak side. (Diagram 19-5.)

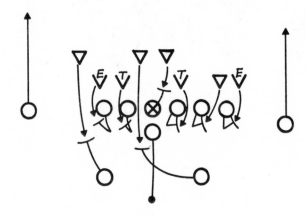

Diagram 19-5

All linemen's blocking remains the same; only the tight end picks up the strong outside linebacker. The split or weakside back blocks the outside weak linebacker, and the strong side offensive back crosses over, behind the drop back passer, and picks up the weakside linebacker. (Diagram 19-5.)

The set back's rule states: Check inside linebacker first, then outside linebacker; and, if no blitz, get into the pass pattern. Therefore, each set back sets off to block first; and if no linebacker blitzes, the set back takes off for a vacated area. Diagram 19-6 illustrates how the backs find the open space in the opposition's pass defense by reading the linebacker's assigned drop back area.

Using the above pass pattern technique, the Veer Pro or Split Pro formation never wastes a blocker by using him to block "shadows." This gives the quarterback a greater number of targets to help pick apart the opposition's pass defense.

Veer or Split Pro Divide Pass

The divide pass as shown in Diagram 19-7 points out the success of throwing in the seam of the three deep zone pass defense. The tight end deep angle pattern, through the head of the safetyman, holds the deep secondary member of his deep middle one third zone. The flanker back's flag out occupies the deep outside one third defender, which enables the circling back to run an open seam pass pattern. (Diagram 19-7.)

The sooner the passer hits the back in the seam, the better, because the deeper the pass, the more zone area the deep defending secondary defenders are able to cover. Thus, this is a bullet-like pass to enable the receiver to catch the ball and take off for the goal line, before the deep defenders are able to recover from their deep zone assignments.

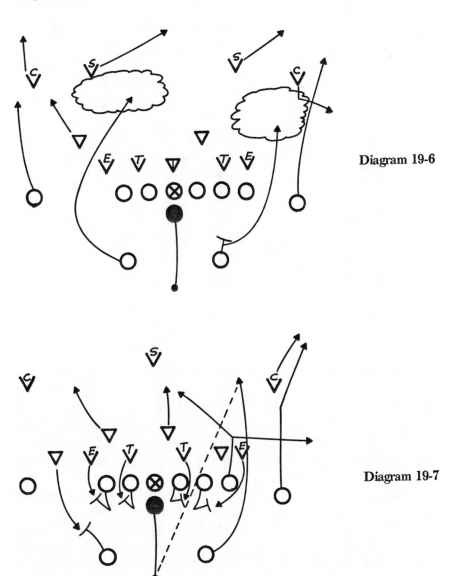

Diagram 19-6

Diagram 19-7

Pro Veer Passing Strategy

Against the three deep pass defense, the quarterback is coached to throw to the flaring back whenever he can isolate the speedy running back against a slower outside linebacker. Diagram 19-8 shows how the halfback can run a swing pattern against the outside linebacker's one-on-one coverage.

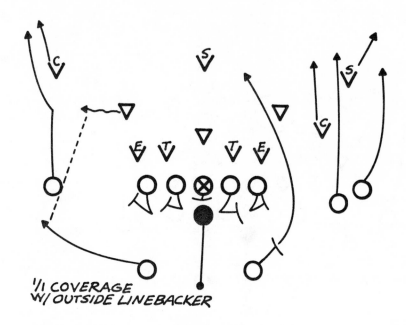

Diagram 19-8

Whenever the secondary plays three deep zone pass defense and the middle safetyman lines up in the deep middle alignment over the head of the offensive center, the quarterback is coached to try to hit the split end with a post pass. This pass is planned to hit the receiver in the middle of the seam between the deep middle safetyman's zone and the deep outside one third zone of the deep outside secondary defender. (Diagram 19-9.)

When the outside pass receiver in the slot alignment is assigned to run an inside cut, the slot man is always taught to run an outside cut. Thus, a curl pattern by the outside receiver tells the slot back to run an out and deep cut. Now the defensive deep defender to the double wide out side is forced to play two pass receivers in his deep outside zone. If he plays the deepest receiver in his area, the curl will

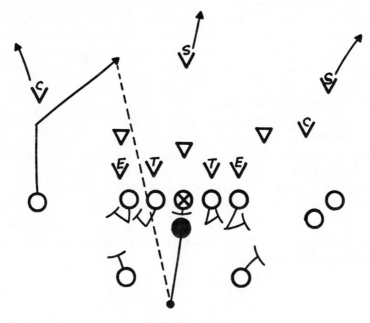

Diagram 19-9

be open. If the deep defender attempts to favor the curl, the quarter-back may hit the slot on his deep up pattern. (Diagram 19-10.)

If the defense fails to double cover the wide slot set, the quarter-back is able to throw quickly to the slot back on or near the line of scrimmage. This allows the slot back to simply run with the ball with the split end as his escort. (Diagram 19-4.)

The swinging slot receiver in Diagram 19-11 must open up to the quarterback so his inside shoulder does not get in the way of the pass. The lead receiver attempts to get the outside angle on the deep secondary defender just as the split end does on his Triple Option run off blocking technique.

Split Divide Pass

The Split Divide Pass is used whenever the defensive team lines up in a balanced alignment. This means that there are five defenders to each side of the center with one defender (middle linebacker) lined up directly on the "center-line" position. (Diagrams 19-12 and 19-13.) Actually, the offensive pass receivers flood the split or weak side of the defensive secondary.

Against the four deep pass defense, the offense runs three deep pass receivers into the split or weak side two deep pass defenders. Both the left split end and left running back take the two deep defenders deep, while the backside running back crosses the offensive formation and runs a deep divide route. This route is run into the seam between the two deep pass defenders to the split or weak side of the offensive formation. (Diagram 19-12.)

Against the three deep secondary, the two split or weak pass receiver (split left and left running back) run their deep pass route versus one and one half secondary defenders. (Deep middle safetyman is referred to as one half a defensive back because his alignment is directly over the center.) The backside running back now runs a deep divide route down the deep seam between the split side deep pass defender and the deep middle safetyman. (Diagram 19-13.)

The pass blockers in both of the Split Divide Pass illustrations assign the tight end to stay in to block to the tight or strong side. The center blocks to the split or weak side because no defender rushes directly over the center.

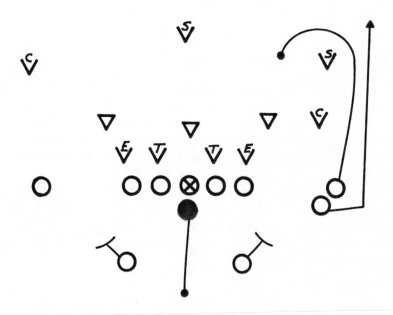

Diagram 19-10

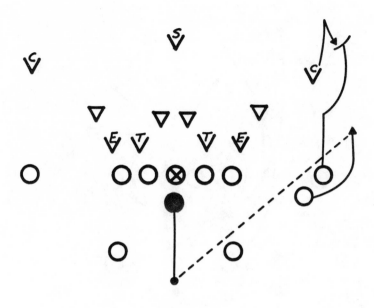

Diagram 19-11

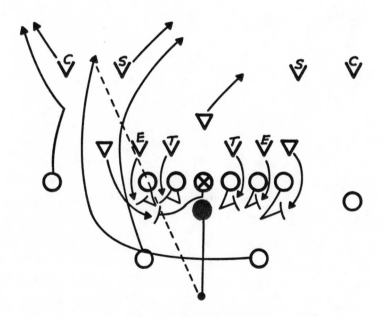

Diagram 19-12

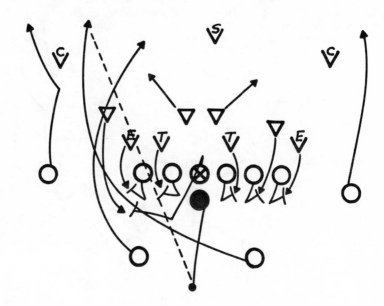

Diagram 19-13

Index